AIR FRYER COOKBOOK
FOR BEGINNERS

2000+ DAYS OF QUICK, HEALTHY, AND DELICIOUS RECIPES FOR FRYING, GRILLING, BAKING, AND CELEBRATORY DISHES. USEFUL TIPS AND TRICKS FOR ALL SKILL LEVELS

Olivia Windrow

🎁 GET YOUR BONUSES!

Scan the QR code to access:

- 5 exclusive bonus recipes
- Photos for every recipe in the book
- Calorie and nutrition data for all dishes

→ oliviawindrow
recipes.com

TABLE OF CONTENT

TABLE OF CONTENT

5 | Air Fryer Fish Feast

6 | Perfect Veggies and Sides

TABLE OF CONTENT

Welcome to the world of culinary exploration with your new air fryer! Whether you are an experienced cook or a beginner, this versatile kitchen assistant promises an exciting journey filled with delightful moments and culinary discoveries. Imagine cooking your favorite dishes, from crispy French fries to golden nuggets, faster and with less oil, making your meals healthier and more enjoyable for you and your family.

Those already familiar with the joys of air frying know the thrill of achieving perfect results with minimal effort. The air fryer has become an indispensable kitchen helper, making cooking more enjoyable and meals healthier.

This book, the "Air Fryer Cookbook for Beginners: 2000+ Days of Quick, Healthy, and Delicious Recipes for Frying, Grilling, Baking, and Celebratory Dishes. Useful Tips and Tricks for All Skill Levels", will be your reliable guide on this exciting culinary adventure. It contains various recipes, from simple everyday meals to sophisticated holiday treats. Discover new techniques and insider tips to enhance the flavor and texture of your dishes with unique spice blends, marinades, and coatings.

Our goal is to make every meal healthier and tastier and elevate your culinary skills. Air fryers represent a true innovation in the kitchen, making cooking faster and healthier than ever before. So, what exactly is an air fryer, and why has it become such a popular appliance?

CHAPTER 1

AIR FRYER HACKS FOR BETTER COOKING

What is an Air Fryer?

An air fryer is a kitchen appliance that is quickly becoming indispensable in many kitchens worldwide. It allows you to enjoy fried foods without the excess fats and calories of traditional frying. This is an excellent solution for those who want to cook healthy meals without sacrificing taste and texture.

How it Works?

An air fryer uses hot air to circulate around the food, creating a crispy crust on the outside while keeping the food tender on the inside. It works similarly to a convection oven, but due to its compact size and powerful heating element, the air fryer heats up much faster and cooks food more evenly. You no longer need to immerse food in oil to achieve the same crispiness, significantly reducing the fat content in your meals.

WHY CHOOSE **AN AIR FRYER?**

1 | *Healthier Cooking:* You can prepare your favorite dishes with minimal or no oil, making your diet healthier.

2 | *Speed and Convenience:* Air fryers heat up faster than conventional ovens and cook food in less time. This is incredibly convenient for busy people who want to prepare delicious meals quickly after a long day.

3 | *Versatility:* In addition to frying, air fryers can bake, grill, defrost, and even roast. Thus, they can be used to cook a wide range of dishes, from French fries and chicken wings to baked goods and grilled vegetables.

4 | *Easy Cleaning:* Removable parts, such as the basket and tray, are easy to wash. Most have a non-stick coating, making the cleaning process quick and straightforward.

5 |*Space-Saving:* The compact size of an air fryer means it takes up little space on your kitchen countertop. It is perfect for small kitchens or apartments.

HOW TO CHOOSE THE RIGHT **AIR FRYER FOR YOUR NEEDS**

1 | *Size and Capacity:* Consider the space on your countertop and the number of people you usually cook for. There are various models with different sizes and capacities. For example, a 5-6 liter air fryer is ideal for a family of four.

2 | *Performance and Settings:* Look for features such as preset programs for different types of food and adjustable temperature settings.

3 | *Ease of Use and Cleaning:* Choose models with intuitive interfaces and easy-to-clean removable parts.

4 | *Safety Features:* Ensure the air fryer has safety features like overheat protection and automatic shut-off.

SETUP AND SAFETY **WHEN USING YOUR AIR FRYER**

Place the air fryer on a heat-resistant surface with adequate ventilation.

Preheat the air fryer if the recipe requires even cooking.

Lightly spray oil on the cooking surface to prevent sticking.

Avoid overcrowding the basket to ensure proper air circulation.

Use suitable cookware to avoid damaging the non-stick coating.

Use oven mitts to handle hot parts.

MAIN FUNCTIONS **AND SETTINGS OF AN AIR FRYER**

Temperature Control: Air fryers usually operate between 180°F to 400°F.

Preset Programs: Many models have preset functions for popular dishes like French fries, chicken, and fish.

Timer Settings: Use the timer to avoid overcooking or undercooking your food.

Accessories: Some air fryers have additional accessories like baking pans and grill racks, expanding their functionality.

INGREDIENT **PREPARATION**

How to Properly Prepare Vegetables for Air Frying

Wash and dry vegetables thoroughly to remove excess moisture, ensuring a crispy texture.

Cut vegetables into even pieces for uniform cooking.

Lightly coat with oil or cooking spray to enhance crispiness.

Blanch certain vegetables, like broccoli, to preserve color and texture.

Meat Preparation Techniques for Optimal Results

Trim excess fat to avoid smoke and splattering.

Marinate meat for added flavor and tenderness.

Use a cooking thermometer to ensure the correct internal temperature.

Consider pounding thick cuts of meat to an even thickness for uniform cooking.

Using Marinades and Spices to Enhance Flavor

Marinate meat and vegetables for at least 30 minutes to enhance flavor.

Use a mix of herbs, spices, and acidic ingredients like lemon juice or vinegar in your marinades.

Pat marinated items dry before cooking to avoid excess moisture and ensure crispiness.

Experiment with spices and dry rubs to create unique flavor profiles.Cooking Techniques

COOKING **TECHNIQUES**

Achieving Crispy Texture Without Excess Oil

Use minimal oil: usually, a light spray or brushing of oil is sufficient.

Preheat the air fryer to ensure immediate heat contact with the food.

Shake or flip food halfway through cooking for even browning.

Optimal Temperature and Time Settings for Various Dishes

Chicken breasts: 370°F for 20-25 minutes

French fries: 400°F for 15-20 minutes

Fish fillets: 390°F for 10-12 minutes

Vegetables: 380°F for 12-15 minutes

Follow specific recipes for exact settings.

Avoiding Overcooking or Drying Out Food

Monitor the cooking process and check food a few minutes before the recommended cooking time.

Use a cooking thermometer to check for doneness.

Avoid cutting meat immediately after cooking; let it rest to retain juices.

CLEANING **AND MAINTENANCE**

Properly Cleaning the Air Fryer After Use

Unplug and let the air fryer cool completely before cleaning.

Remove and wash the basket, tray, and other removable parts with warm soapy water.

Wipe the interior and exterior with a damp cloth.

Avoid abrasive sponges that can damage the non-stick coating.

Tips for Keeping Your Air Fryer in Excellent Condition

Regularly check and remove food debris from the heating element.

Inspect for wear and tear, such as cracks in the basket or worn trays, and replace if necessary.

Store in a cool, dry place when not in use to prevent damage.

Using Eco-Friendly Cleaning Products

Use mild detergents and natural cleaners.

Avoid harsh chemicals that can damage the appliance and harm the environment.

Thoroughly dry all parts before reassembling to prevent mold and mildew.

By following these tips and techniques, you can make the most of your air fryer and ensure delicious and healthy meals every time.

AIR FRYER **COOKING GUIDE**

Dish	Temperature °F (°C)	Cooking Time	Notes
French Fries	400°F (200°C)	15-20 minutes	Shake halfway through
Chicken Wings	375°F (190°C)	25-30 minutes	Turn halfway through
Fish Sticks	400°F (200°C)	10-12 minutes	Turn halfway through
Mozzarella Sticks	375°F (190°C)	8-10 minutes	Watch for cheese melting
Chicken Breasts	375°F (190°C)	20-25 minutes	Turn halfway through
Roasted Vegetables	400°F (200°C)	10-15 minutes	Stir once
Pork Chops	400°F (200°C)	12-15 minutes	Turn halfway through
Salmon Fillet	375°F (190°C)	10-12 minutes	Do not turn
Loaded Nachos	350°F (175°C)	5-7 minutes	Watch for cheese melting
Beef Steak	400°F (200°C)	10-12 minutes	Turn halfway through
Sweet Potatoes	370°F (190°C)	20-25 minutes	Turn halfway through
Frozen Burgers	375°F (190°C)	12-15 minutes	Turn halfway through
Breaded Shrimp	400°F (200°C)	8-10 minutes	Watch for golden crust
Loaded Potato Skins	370°F (190°C)	15-20 minutes	Turn halfway through
Stuffed Mushrooms	375°F (190°C)	15-20 minutes	Monitor doneness
Stuffed Peppers	375°F (190°C)	20-25 minutes	Monitor pepper softness
Frozen Chicken Nuggets	400°F (200°C)	10-12 minutes	Shake halfway through

Dish	Temperature °F (°C)	Cooking Time	Notes
Frozen Pizza	360°F (180°C)	8-12 minutes	Watch for cheese melting
Cheesecake	350°F (175°C)	20-25 minutes	Check with a toothpick
Frozen Pies	350°F (175°C)	15-20 minutes	Cook until golden brown
Crispy Bacon	400°F (200°C)	8-10 minutes	Watch for crispiness
Brussels Sprouts	375°F (190°C)	15-20 minutes	Shake halfway through
Frozen Bagels with Cream Cheese	350°F (175°C)	10-12 minutes	Cook until golden brown
Popcorn	400°F (200°C)	8-10 minutes	Shake basket every few minutes
Muffins	320°F (160°C	12-15 minutes	Check with a toothpick

This table is a general guide and may vary depending on the brand of the air fryer and portion sizes. Monitor your food while cooking and adjust the time and temperature as needed.

CHAPTER 2

MORNING FAVORITE

ULTIMATE CRISPY BACON

● INGREDIENTS 🍽 YIELDS | 4 SERVES

8 slices of thick-cut bacon

● DIRECTIONS ⏱ PREP TIME | 5 MIN 🔲 COOK TIME | 10 MIN

1 | Preheat your air fryer to 400°F (204°C) for about 5 minutes.
2 | Place the bacon slices in a single layer in the air fryer basket. Ensure the slices do not overlap even when cooking.
3 | Air fry the bacon at 400° (204°C) F for 10 minutes.

CRISPY AVOCADO FRIES

● INGREDIENTS 🍽 YIELDS | 4 SERVES

2 large avocados, ripe but firm
1/2 cup all-purpose flour
2 large eggs
1 cup panko breadcrumbs

1/2 teaspoon garlic powder
1/2 teaspoon smoked paprika
1/2 teaspoon salt
1/4 teaspoon black pepper
Cooking spray

● DIRECTIONS ⏱ PREP TIME | 10 MIN 🔲 COOK TIME | 10 MIN

1 | Preheat the air fryer to 400°F (200°C) for about 5 minutes.
2 | Cut the avocados in half, remove the pit, and slice each half into 4-6 wedges, depending on the size of the avocado.
3 | Place the flour in a shallow dish. Beat the eggs in another shallow dish. Combine the panko breadcrumbs, garlic powder, smoked paprika, salt, and black pepper in a third shallow dish.
4 | Dredge each avocado wedge in the flour, shaking off any excess. Dip in the beaten eggs, then coat with the seasoned panko breadcrumbs, pressing gently to adhere.
5 | Lightly spray the air fryer basket with cooking spray. Arrange the avocado wedges in a single layer in the basket, ensuring they do not overlap.
6 | Cook in the preheated air fryer for 10 minutes, flipping halfway through, until the avocado fries are golden brown and crispy.
7 | Serve immediately with your favorite dipping sauce, ranch, aioli, or salsa.

PERFECT **VFRENCH TOAST**

● **INGREDIENTS** 🍽 **YIELDS** | 4 SERVES

4 slices of thick-cut bread
2 large eggs
1/2 cup whole milk
1 teaspoon vanilla extract

1 teaspoon ground cinnamon
1/4 teaspoon ground nutmeg
2 tablespoons granulated sugar
Cooking spray

● **DIRECTIONS** ⏱ PREP TIME | 10 MIN 🍳 COOK TIME | 8 MIN

1 | Preheat your air fryer to 370°F (188°C) for about 5 minutes.
2 | Cut each slice of bread into 3 sticks.
3 | In a large bowl, whisk together the eggs, milk, vanilla extract, cinnamon, nutmeg, and sugar.
4 | Dip each breadstick into the egg mixture. Make sure it is completely covered. Let the excess run off.
5 | Lightly spray the air fryer basket with cooking spray. Place the coated bread sticks in the air fryer basket in a single layer. Cook at 370°F (188°C) for 8 minutes, turning halfway through, until golden brown and crispy.

CRISPY **BREAKFAST POTATOES**

● **INGREDIENTS** 🍽 **YIELDS** | 4 SERVES

1 pound russet potatoes
1 tablespoon olive oil
1 teaspoon garlic powder
1 teaspoon onion powder

1 teaspoon paprika
1/2 teaspoon salt
1/4 teaspoon black pepper
1/4 teaspoon dried rosemary (optional)
Cooking spray

● **DIRECTIONS** ⏱ PREP TIME | 20 MIN 🍳 COOK TIME | 1 MIN

1 | Preheat the air fryer to 400°F (204°C) for about 5 minutes.
2 | Wash and dice the potatoes into 1/2-inch cubes.
3 | In a large bowl, toss the diced potatoes with olive oil, garlic powder, onion powder, paprika, salt, black pepper, and rosemary if using.
4 | Lightly spray the air fryer basket with cooking spray. Place the seasoned potatoes in a single layer in the air fryer basket.
5 | Cook at 400°F for 20 minutes, shaking the basket halfway through for even cooking until the potatoes are golden brown and crispy.

FLUFFY **HOMEMADE DONUTS**

● INGREDIENTS 🥞 YIELDS | 4 SERVES

1 can (16.3 oz) refrigerated biscuit dough
1/4 cup granulated sugar

1 teaspoon ground cinnamon
2 tablespoons melted butter
Cooking spray

● DIRECTIONS ⏱ PREP TIME | 15 MIN 🔲 COOK TIME | 10MIN

1 | Preheat the air fryer to 350°F (175°C) for about 5 minutes.
2 | Separate the biscuit dough and use a small round cutter to make a hole in the center of each biscuit to form donut shapes.
3 | Lightly spray the air fryer basket with cooking spray. Place the donuts in a single layer in the air fryer basket.
4 | Cook at 350°F (175°C) for 8-10 minutes or until golden brown, flipping halfway through.
5 | While the donuts are cooking, mix the granulated sugar and cinnamon in a bowl. Grease the finished donuts with melted butter and dip them in the sugar and cinnamon mixture.
6 | Grease the finished donuts with melted butter and dip them in the sugar and cinnamon mixture.

LOADED **BREAKFAST BURRITOS**

● INGREDIENTS 🥞 YIELDS | 4 SERVES

4 large flour tortillas
4 large eggs
1/2 cup shredded cheddar cheese
1/2 cup cooked and crumbled breakfast sausage or bacon
1/4 cup diced bell pepper

1/4 cup diced onion
1/4 cup salsa
1/4 cup sour cream
Cooking spray
Salt and pepper to taste

● DIRECTIONS ⏱ PREP TIME | 15 MIN 🔲 COOK TIME | 10 MIN

1 | Preheat the air fryer to 350°F (175°C) for about 5 minutes.
2 | In a skillet, scramble the eggs with salt and pepper until fully cooked.
3 | Lay out the tortillas and evenly distribute the scrambled eggs, cooked sausage or bacon, shredded cheddar cheese, diced bell pepper, diced onion, and salsa in the center of each tortilla.
4 | Roll up the tortillas burrito-style by folding in the sides and then rolling from the bottom up. Lightly spray the outside of each burrito with cooking spray.
5 | Place the burritos in the air fryer basket seam-side down. Cook at 350°F (175°C) for 5-7 minutes or until the tortillas are golden brown and crispy. Serve with sour cream.

GOLDEN **HASH BROWNS**

● **INGREDIENTS** 🍽 YIELDS | 4 SERVES

4 medium russet potatoes
1 small onion, finely diced
1 teaspoon salt
1/2 teaspoon black pepper

1/2 teaspoon garlic powder
1/2 teaspoon paprika
2 tablespoons olive oil
1 large egg
Cooking spray

● **DIRECTIONS** 🕐 PREP TIME | 10 MIN 📟 COOK TIME | 20 MIN

1 | Preheat the air fryer to 375°F (190°C) for about 5 minutes.
2 | Peel and grate the potatoes. Rinse the grated potatoes under cold water and squeeze out as much moisture as possible using a clean kitchen towel or paper towel.
3 | Combine the grated potatoes, finely diced onion, salt, black pepper, garlic powder, paprika, olive oil, and egg in a large bowl. Mix until well combined.
4 | Lightly spray the air fryer basket with cooking spray. Form the potato mixture into small patties and place them in a single layer in the air fryer basket.
5 | Cook at 375°F (190°C) for 10 minutes. Flip the hash browns and cook for 10 minutes until golden brown and crispy.

SAVORY **SAUSAGE PATTIES**

● **INGREDIENTS** 🍽 YIELDS | 4 SERVES

1 pound ground pork
1 teaspoon salt
1/2 teaspoon black pepper
1 teaspoon dried sage
1/2 teaspoon dried thyme

1/2 teaspoon garlic powder
1/2 teaspoon onion powder
1/4 teaspoon crushed red pepper
flakes (optional)
Cooking spray

● **DIRECTIONS** 🕐 PREP TIME | 10 MIN 📟 COOK TIME | 12 MIN

1 | In a large bowl, combine the ground pork, salt, black pepper, dried sage, dried thyme, garlic powder, onion powder, and crushed red pepper flakes (if using). Mix until well combined.
2 | Form the pork mixture into 8 equal-sized patties.
3 | Preheat the air fryer to 375°F (190°C) for about 5 minutes.
4 | Lightly spray the air fryer basket with cooking spray. Place the sausage patties in a single layer in the air fryer basket.
5 | Cook at 375°F (190°C) for 12 minutes, flipping halfway through, or until the sausage patties are fully cooked and golden brown.

FLUFFY **OMELETTE DELIGHT**

● INGREDIENTS  YIELDS | 4 SERVES

4 large eggs
1/4 cup whole milk
1/2 cup shredded cheddar cheese
1/4 teaspoon salt

1/4 cup diced bell pepper
1/4 cup diced onion
1/4 cup diced ham or cooked bacon
1/4 teaspoon black pepper
Cooking spray

● DIRECTIONS 🕐 PREP TIME | 10 MIN COOK TIME | 10 MIN

1 | Preheat the air fryer to 350°F (175°C) for about 5 minutes.
2 | In a large bowl, whisk together the eggs, milk salt, and black pepper until well combined.
3 | Lightly spray an air fryer-safe baking dish or small cake pan with cooking spray. Pour the egg mixture into the dish.
4 | Evenly distribute the diced bell pepper, diced onion, diced ham or cooked bacon, and shredded cheddar cheese over the egg mixture.
5 | Place the dish in the air fryer basket and cook at 350°F (175°C) for 10 minutes or until the omelet is set and cooked through.

BURSTING **BLUEBERRY MUFFINS**

● INGREDIENTS YIELDS | 4 SERVES

1 cup all-purpose flour
1/2 cup granulated sugar
1/2 teaspoon baking powder
1/4 teaspoon baking soda
1/4 teaspoon salt

1/2 cup whole milk
1/4 cup vegetable oil
1 large egg
1 teaspoon vanilla extract
1 cup fresh blueberries
Cooking spray

● DIRECTIONS 🕐 PREP TIME | 10 MIN COOK TIME | 15 MIN

1 | Whisk together the flour, sugar, baking powder, baking soda, and salt
in a large bowl.
2 | Whisk together the milk, vegetable oil, egg, and vanilla extract in a separate bowl until well combined.
3 | Pour the wet ingredients into the dry ingredients and stir until just combined. Fold in the blueberries.
4 | Lightly spray silicone cups or an air fryer-safe muffin tin with cooking spray. Fill each cup about 2/3 full with the muffin batter.
5 | Preheat the air fryer to 350°F (175°C) for about 5 minutes.
6 | Place the muffin cups in the air fryer basket and cook at 350°F (175°C) for 12-15 minutes, or until a toothpick inserted into the center of a muffin comes out clean.

GOURMET **AVOCADO TOAST**

● **INGREDIENTS** 🥞 YIELDS | 4 SERVES

4 slices of whole-grain bread
2 ripe avocados
1 tablespoon lemon juice
1/2 teaspoon salt

1/4 teaspoon black pepper
1/4 teaspoon red pepper flakes
(optional)
1/4 cup crumbled feta cheese
1/4 cup cherry tomatoes, halved
Cooking spray

● **DIRECTIONS** ⏱ PREP TIME | 10 MIN 📟 COOK TIME | 5 MIN

1 | Preheat the air fryer to 370°F (188°C) for about 5 minutes.
2 | Lightly spray both sides of the bread slices with cooking spray. Place the bread slices in the air fryer basket.
3 | Cook at 370°F (188°C) for 3-5 minutes or until the bread is golden brown and crispy.
4 | While the bread is toasting, scoop the avocado flesh into a bowl and mash it with a fork. Stir in the lemon juice, salt, black pepper, and red pepper flakes if using.
5 | Spread the mashed avocado mixture evenly over the toasted bread. Top with crumbled feta cheese and cherry tomato halves.

TENDER **CINNAMON ROLLS**

● **INGREDIENTS** 🥞 YIELDS | 4 SERVES

1 can (8 oz) refrigerated crescent roll
dough
1/4 cup unsalted butter, melted
1/3 cup granulated sugar

2 teaspoons ground cinnamon
1/4 cup brown sugar
1/4 cup chopped pecans (optional)
Cooking spray

● **DIRECTIONS** ⏱ PREP TIME | 15 MIN 📟 COOK TIME | 10 MIN

1 | Roll out the crescent roll dough flat, pressing the seams together to form a single sheet. Brush the melted butter evenly over the dough.
2 | Mix the granulated sugar, ground cinnamon, and brown sugar in a small bowl. Sprinkle the mixture evenly over the buttered dough and top with chopped pecans.
3 | Roll the dough tightly into a log shape, starting from one of the shorter ends. Cut the log into 8 equal slices to form the cinnamon rolls.
4 | Lightly spray the air fryer basket with cooking spray. Place the cinnamon rolls in the basket in a single layer.
5 | Preheat the air fryer to 350°F (175°C) for about 5 minutes.
6 | Place the basket with the cinnamon rolls in the preheated air fryer. Cook at 350°F (175°C) for 8-10 minutes or until golden brown and cooked through.

PROTEIN **EGG BITES**

● INGREDIENTS  YIELDS | 4 SERVES

6 large eggs
1/2 cup cottage cheese
1/4 cup shredded cheddar cheese
1/4 cup diced bell pepper

1/4 cup diced cooked bacon or ham
1/4 teaspoon salt
1/4 teaspoon black pepper
Cooking spray

● DIRECTIONS ⏱ PREP TIME | 10 MIN 🍳 COOK TIME | 12 MIN

1 | Combine the eggs, cottage cheese, salt, and black pepper until smooth.
2 | Lightly spray silicone cups or an air fryer-safe muffin tin with cooking spray. Pour the egg mixture evenly into the cups, filling them about halfway.
3 | Evenly distribute the diced bell pepper and cooked bacon or ham among the cups, then sprinkle with shredded cheddar cheese.
4 | Preheat the air fryer to 300°F (150°C) for about 5 minutes.
5 | Place the muffin cups in the preheated air fryer basket and cook at 300°F (150°C) for 12 minutes or until the egg bites are set and cooked.

CLASSIC **FLUFFY PANCAKES**

● INGREDIENTS   YIELDS | 4 SERVES

1 cup all-purpose flour
2 tablespoons granulated sugar
1 teaspoon baking powder
1/2 teaspoon baking soda
1/4 teaspoon salt

3/4 cup buttermilk
1/4 cup whole milk
1 large egg
2 tablespoons unsalted butter, melted
Cooking spray

● DIRECTIONS ⏱ PREP TIME | 10 MIN 🍳 COOK TIME | 8 MIN

1 | Whisk together the flour, sugar, baking powder, baking soda, and salt
in a large bowl.
2 | Whisk together the buttermilk, whole milk, egg, and melted butter in a separate bowl until well combined.
3 | Pour the wet ingredients into the dry ingredients and stir until just combined, being careful not to overmix.
4 | Lightly spray silicone muffin cups or an air fryer-safe baking dish with cooking spray. Pour the pancake batter into the cups or dish, filling about halfway.
5 | Preheat the air fryer to 350°F (175°C) for about 5 minutes.
6 | Place the filled muffin cups or baking dish in the preheated air fryer. Cook at 350°F (175°C) for 8 minutes or until the pancakes are fluffy and cooked through.

SWEET **BANANA BREAD**

● **INGREDIENTS** 🍽 YIELDS | 4 SERVES

1 cup all-purpose flour
1/2 teaspoon baking soda
1/4 teaspoon salt
1/2 cup granulated sugar
1/4 cup unsalted butter, melted
1 large egg

1/4 cup whole milk
1 teaspoon vanilla extract
2 ripe bananas, mashed
1/4 cup chopped walnuts (optional)
Cooking spray

● **DIRECTIONS** ⏱ PREP TIME | 10 MIN 🍳 COOK TIME | 25 MIN

1 | Whisk together the flour, baking soda, and salt in a large bowl.
2 | In a separate bowl, mix the sugar and melted butter. Add the egg, milk, and vanilla extract and mix until well combined. Stir in the mashed bananas.
3 | Gradually add the wet ingredients to the dry ingredients and mix until combined. If using, fold in the chopped walnuts.
4 | Lightly spray an air fryer-safe loaf pan with cooking spray. Pour the batter into the loaf pan and smooth the top.
5 | Preheat the air fryer to 320°F (160°C) for about 5 minutes.
6 | Place the loaf pan in the preheated air fryer. Cook at 320°F (160°C) for 25 minutes or until a toothpick inserted into the center comes clean.

BACON **BREAKFAST DOGS**

● **INGREDIENTS** 🍽 YIELDS | 4 SERVES

4 hot dogs
4 slices of bacon
4 hot dog buns

1/4 cup shredded cheddar cheese (optional)
Mustard and ketchup (optional)

● **DIRECTIONS** ⏱ PREP TIME | 10 MIN 🍳 COOK TIME | 15 MIN

1 | Preheat the air fryer to 375°F (190°C).
2 | Wrap each hot dog with a slice of bacon, securing it with toothpicks if necessary.
3 | Place the bacon-wrapped hot dogs in the air fryer basket, ensuring they are not touching.
4 | Cook for 10-12 minutes, turning halfway through, until the bacon is crispy. Remove the toothpicks, place the hot dogs in buns, and top with shredded cheddar cheese, mustard, and ketchup if desired.

ULTIMATE **BREAKFAST SANDWICH**

● **INGREDIENTS**  **YIELDS** | 4 SERVES

4 English muffins, split
4 large eggs
4 slices of cheddar cheese
4 slices of cooked bacon

4 sausage patties
1 tablespoon butter, melted
Salt and pepper to taste
Cooking spray

● **DIRECTIONS** ⏱ **PREP TIME** | 10 MIN 🍳 **COOK TIME** | 15 MIN

1 | Preheat the air fryer to 350°F (175°C) for about 5 minutes.
2 | Lightly spray the air fryer basket with cooking spray. Place the sausage patties in the basket and cook at 350°F (175°C) for 8 minutes, flipping halfway through, until fully cooked.
3 | While the sausage patties are cooking, lightly toast the English muffins in the air fryer for about 2 minutes until golden brown.
4 | In a small bowl, whisk the eggs with salt and pepper. Pour the eggs into an air fryer-safe dish or silicone muffin cups. Cook in the air fryer at 300°F (150°C) for 5 minutes or until set.
5 | Assemble the sandwiches by layering a slice of cheese, a sausage patty, an egg, and a slice of bacon between the English muffin halves. Brush the top of the muffins with melted butter. Place the assembled sandwiches back into the air fryer and cook at 350°F (175°C) for 2-3 minutes to melt the cheese.

CHEESY **VEGGIE BAGELS**

● **INGREDIENTS** **YIELDS** | 2 TO 4 SERVES

2 bagels, halved
1 cup shredded cheddar cheese
1/2 cup chopped bell peppers
1/2 cup chopped spinach

1/4 cup chopped red onion
1/4 cup chopped tomatoes
1 tablespoon olive oil
Salt and pepper to taste

● **DIRECTIONS** ⏱ **PREP TIME** | 15 MIN 🍳 **COOK TIME** | 10 MIN

1 | In a bowl, mix the chopped bell peppers, spinach, red onion, and tomatoes with olive oil. Season with salt and pepper to taste.
2 | Spread the vegetable mixture evenly on the cut sides of the bagels.
3 | Sprinkle shredded cheddar cheese over the vegetables.
4 | Place the bagel halves in the air fryer basket.
5 | Cook at 350°F (175°C) for 8-10 minutes. So that the cheese melts and the bagels become crispy.

CHEESY BREAKFAST QUESADILLA

● INGREDIENTS 🍳 YIELDS | 4 SERVES

4 large flour tortillas
6 large eggs
1/2 cup shredded cheddar cheese
1/2 cup shredded Monterey Jack
cheese

1/4 cup diced bell pepper
1/4 cup diced onion
1/4 cup cooked and crumbled bacon
Salt and pepper to taste
Cooking spray

● DIRECTIONS ⏱ PREP TIME | 10 MIN 🍳 COOK TIME | 8 MIN

1 | In a medium bowl, whisk the eggs with salt and pepper. Lightly spray a non-stick skillet with cooking spray and scramble the eggs over medium heat until fully cooked. Remove from heat and set aside.
2 | Lay out the flour tortillas and evenly distribute the scrambled eggs, bell pepper, diced onion, cooked bacon, and shredded cheese over half of each tortilla. Fold the other half of the tortilla over the filling to create a half-moon shape.
3 | Lightly spray the air fryer basket with cooking spray. Place the quesadillas in the basket, making sure they do not overlap.
4 | Preheat the air fryer to 350°F (175°C) for about 5 minutes.
5 | Place the basket with the quesadillas in the preheated air fryer. Cook at 350°F (175°C) for 4 minutes, then carefully flip the quesadillas and cook for another 4 minutes until the tortillas are golden brown and the cheese has melted.

ENERGIZING GRANOLA BALLS

● INGREDIENTS 🍳 YIELDS | 2 TO 4 SERVES

1 cup rolled oats
1/2 cup peanut butter
1/4 cup honey
1/4 cup dark chocolate chips

1/4 cup chopped nuts (such as
almonds or walnuts)
1/4 cup dried cranberries or raisins
1 teaspoon vanilla extract
1/2 teaspoon cinnamon

● DIRECTIONS ⏱ PREP TIME | 15 MIN 🍳 COOK TIME | 10 MIN

1 | In a large mixing bowl, Combine oats, peanut butter, honey, chocolate chips, nuts, dried cranberries (or raisins), vanilla extract, and cinnamon. Mix all ingredients until evenly distributed.
2 | Roll the mixture into small balls about 1 inch in diameter.
3 | Place the granola balls in the air fryer basket.
4 | Cook at 325°F (160°C) for 8-10 minutes or until the granola balls are slightly browned and firm.
5 | Let the granola balls cool before serving.

SOUTHERN-STYLE BISCUITS

● INGREDIENTS 🥞 YIELDS | 4 SERVES

2 cups all-purpose flour
1 tablespoon baking powder
1/2 teaspoon baking soda
1 teaspoon salt

1/2 cup cold unsalted butter, cubed
3/4 cup buttermilk
1 tablespoon melted butter for
brushing
Cooking spray

● DIRECTIONS ⏱ PREP TIME | 15 MIN 🍳 COOK TIME | 10 MIN

1 | Whisk together the flour, baking powder, baking soda, and salt in a large bowl.
2 | Cut in the cold butter using a pastry cutter or fingers until the mixture resembles coarse crumbs. Stir in the buttermilk until just combined, being careful not to overmix.
3 | Turn the dough onto a lightly floured surface and knead gently until smooth. Pat the dough out to a 1/2-inch thickness. Cut out biscuits using a biscuit cutter or a round cookie cutter.
4 | Lightly spray the air fryer basket with cooking spray. Place the biscuits in the basket, making sure they do not touch.
5 | Preheat the air fryer to 375°F (190°C) for about 5 minutes.
6 | Place the basket with the biscuits in the preheated air fryer. Bake at 375°F (190°C) for 10 minutes until golden brown. Brush the tops with melted butter.

APPLE CINNAMON MUFFINS

● INGREDIENTS 🥞 YIELDS | 4 SERVES

1 cup all-purpose flour
1/2 cup granulated sugar
1/2 teaspoon baking powder
1/4 teaspoon baking soda
1/4 teaspoon salt
1/2 teaspoon ground cinnamon

1/4 cup unsalted butter, melted
1/2 cup buttermilk
1 large egg
1 teaspoon vanilla extract
1 medium apple, peeled, cored, and
finely chopped

● DIRECTIONS ⏱ PREP TIME | 15 MIN 🍳 COOK TIME | 12 MIN

1 | Mix flour, sugar, baking powder, soda, salt, and cinnamon
in a large bowl.
2 | Mix melted butter, buttermilk, egg, and vanilla extract in another bowl until well combined.
3 | Add the wet ingredients to the dry ingredients and mix until just combined. Fold in the chopped apple.
4 | Divide the batter evenly among 4 silicone muffin molds (4-ounce capacity each). Place the molds in the air fryer basket.
5 | Set the air fryer to 350°F and cook for 12 minutes or until a toothpick inserted into the center of a muffin comes out clean.

CHEDDAR **MORNING SOUFFLES**

● **INGREDIENTS** ☰ YIELDS | 4 SERVES

4 large eggs
1/2 cup milk
1/4 teaspoon salt
1/4 teaspoon black pepper
1 cup shredded cheddar cheese
1/4 cup grated Parmesan cheese

1/2 teaspoon garlic powder
1/2 teaspoon onion powder
1/2 teaspoon dried thyme
2 tablespoons butter, melted
4 large flour tortillas
Cooking spray

● **DIRECTIONS** ⏱ PREP TIME | 12 MIN 🍳 COOK TIME | 10 MIN

1 | In a large bowl, whisk together the eggs, milk, salt, black pepper, garlic powder, onion powder, and dried thyme until well combined.
2 | Gently fold the shredded cheddar cheese and grate Parmesan cheese into the egg mixture.
3 | Preheat the air fryer to 375°F (190°C) and spray four small oven-safe ramekins with cooking spray. Divide the melted butter among the ramekins, coating the bottom and sides.
4 | Pour the egg and cheese mixture evenly into the prepared ramekins. Place the ramekins in the air fryer basket.
5 | Cook the souffles in the air fryer for 10-12 minutes or until they are puffed up and golden brown on top. Serve immediately with warm, lightly toasted flour tortillas on the side.

FRIED **EGG SANDWICH**

● **INGREDIENTS** ☰ YIELDS | 4 SERVES

4 large eggs
4 slices of bread
4 slices of cheddar cheese

1 tbsp butter, softened
Salt and pepper to taste
Cooking spray

● **DIRECTIONS** ⏱ PREP TIME | 5 MIN 🍳 COOK TIME | 8 MIN

1 | Preheat the air fryer to 350°F. Lightly spray the air fryer basket with cooking spray.
2 | Lightly grease ramekins or silicone molds with cooking spray. Crack an egg into each ramekin, season with salt and pepper, and place them in the air fryer basket. Cook at 350°F for 5-6 minutes until the eggs harden to your liking.
3 | Butter one side of each bread slice. Place the bread slices, butter side down, in the air fryer basket. Top with a slice of cheese and the cooked egg.
4 | Top with another slice of bread, butter side up.
5 | Cook at 350°F for 3-4 minutes. The bread should turn golden brown, and the cheese should melt. Turn halfway through cooking time.
6 | Serve immediately.

FLUFFY **FRITTATA DELIGHT**

● INGREDIENTS ⬡ YIELDS | 4 SERVES

6 large eggs
1/2 cup milk
1 cup diced bell peppers (any color)
1/2 cup diced onions

1 cup spinach leaves, chopped
1 cup shredded cheese (cheddar or
your favorite blend)
Salt and pepper to taste
1 tablespoon olive oil

● DIRECTIONS ⏱ PREP TIME | 10 MIN ⬡ COOK TIME | 20 MIN

1 | Whisk the eggs and milk in a large bowl until well combined—season with salt and pepper.
2 | Heat olive oil in a skillet over medium heat. Add diced bell peppers and onions, cooking until softened, about 5 minutes. Add chopped spinach and cook for another 2 minutes.
3 | Pour the vegetable mixture into the egg mixture, add shredded cheese, and stir to combine.
4 | Pour the mixture into an air fryer-safe baking dish.
5 | Preheat the air fryer to 350°F (175°C) for about 5 minutes.
6 | Place the dish with the frittata mixture in the preheated air fryer. Cook for 18-20 minutes until the frittata is golden brown. Let it cool slightly before slicing and serving.

BANANA-NUT **FRENCH TOAST**

● INGREDIENTS ⬡ YIELDS | 4 SERVES

4 slices of thick-cut bread
2 large eggs
1/2 cup milk
1 teaspoon vanilla extract

1/2 teaspoon ground cinnamon
1 ripe banana, mashed
1/4 cup chopped walnuts
Cooking spray or oil

● DIRECTIONS ⏱ PREP TIME | 10 MIN ⬡ COOK TIME | 15 MIN

1 | Whisk together the eggs, milk, vanilla extract, and ground cinnamon in a large bowl until well combined.
2 | Stir in the mashed banana and chopped walnuts.
3 | Dip each slice of bread into the egg mixture. Make sure it is completely covered.
4 | Preheat the air fryer to 350°F (175°C) for about 5 minutes.
5 | Lightly grease the air fryer basket with cooking spray or oil. Place the coated bread slices into the basket in a single layer.
6 | Cook for 10-12 minutes, flipping halfway through, until the French toast is golden brown and crispy. Remove from the air fryer and let cool slightly before serving.

SWEET **POTATO HASH**

● **INGREDIENTS** ⬚ YIELDS | 4 SERVES

2 large sweet potatoes, peeled and
diced
1 red bell pepper, diced
1 green bell pepper, diced
1 small onion, diced

2 tablespoons olive oil
1 teaspoon garlic powder
1 teaspoon paprika
1/2 teaspoon salt
1/2 teaspoon black pepper

● **DIRECTIONS** ⏱ PREP TIME | 10 MIN ▦ COOK TIME | 20 MIN

1 | Combine the sweet potatoes, red bell pepper, green bell pepper, and onion in a large bowl.
Drizzle with olive oil and toss to coat.
2 | Sprinkle the garlic powder, paprika, salt, and black pepper over the vegetable mixture and toss
again to distribute the seasonings evenly.
3 | Preheat the air fryer to 375°F (190°C) for about 5 minutes. Lightly grease the basket of the air
fryer with cooking spray.
4 | Place the seasoned vegetable mixture in the air fryer basket. Cook in batches if necessary to
avoid overcrowding.
5 | Cook for 15-20 minutes, shaking the basket halfway through, until the sweet potatoes are
tender and slightly crispy on the edges. Serve warm.

MAPLE **PECAN OATMEAL**

● **INGREDIENTS** ⬚ YIELDS | 4 SERVES

1 cup rolled oats
2 cups water or milk
1/4 cup pure maple syrup
1/4 cup chopped pecans

1/2 teaspoon ground cinnamon
1/4 teaspoon salt
1/4 teaspoon vanilla extract
Fresh fruit for topping (optional)

● **DIRECTIONS** ⏱ PREP TIME | 5 MIN ▦ COOK TIME | 15 MIN

1 | Preheat the air fryer to 375°F (190°C).
2 | Combine the rolled oats, water or milk, ground cinnamon, and salt in an oven-safe dish in your
air fryer basket.
3 | Place the dish in the preheated air fryer and cook for 10-12 minutes, stirring halfway through,
until the oats are cooked and have absorbed most of the liquid.
4 | Stir in the maple syrup, chopped pecans, and vanilla extract.
5 | Cook for 2-3 minutes to allow the flavors to meld.
6 | Remove the dish from the air fryer and let it cool slightly.
7 | Top with fresh fruit if desired.

BRITISH **BREAKFAST CLASSIC**

● **INGREDIENTS**   🍽 YIELDS | 4 SERVES

4 sausages
4 slices of bacon
4 eggs
4 tomatoes, halved

1 cup mushrooms, sliced
4 slices of bread
Salt and pepper to taste
Butter for spreading

● **DIRECTIONS**   ⏱ PREP TIME | 15 MIN   🍴 COOK TIME | 20 MIN

1 | Preheat the air fryer to 375°F (190°C).
2 | Place the sausages and bacon in the air fryer basket and cook for 10-12 minutes, turning halfway through until crispy and browned.
3 | Add the tomatoes and mushrooms to the air fryer basket and cook for 5-7 minutes until tender.
4 | While the sausages, bacon, tomatoes, and mushrooms are cooking, toast the bread slices in a toaster or the air fryer until golden brown. Spread butter on each slice.
5 | Using a silicone mold, scramble the eggs on a non-stick stove or deep fryer. The whites should harden, and cook the yolks to your taste: salt and pepper.
6 | Arrange the sausages, bacon, tomatoes, and mushrooms on a plate to serve. Place the fried eggs on top of the mushrooms. Add the buttered toast slices on the side.

BRUNCH **PIZZA DELIGHT**

● **INGREDIENTS**   🍽 YIELDS | 4 SERVES

1 pre-made pizza crust (or flatbread)
4 large eggs
1/2 cup shredded mozzarella cheese
1/4 cup cooked bacon, crumbled
1/4 cup cherry tomatoes, halved

1/4 cup baby spinach, chopped
Salt and pepper to taste
Fresh basil leaves for garnish
(optional)

● **DIRECTIONS**   ⏱ PREP TIME | 10 MIN   🍴 COOK TIME | 10 MIN

1 | Preheat the air fryer to 375°F (190°C).
2 | Place the pizza crust or flatbread in the air fryer basket.
3 | Crack the eggs into a bowl and whisk them with salt and pepper.
4 | Pour the egg mixture over the pizza crust, spreading it evenly.
5 | Sprinkle shredded mozzarella cheese over the egg mixture.
6 | Add the crumbled bacon, cherry tomatoes, and chopped spinach evenly over the top. **7 |** Fry in the air for 8-10 minutes. The eggs should harden, and the cheese should melt and become bubbly.
8 | Remove the breakfast pizza from the air fryer and garnish with fresh basil leaves if desired.

CHAPTER 3

DELICIOUS POULTRY DISHES

CLASSIC **BUTTERMILK FRIED CHICKEN**

● INGREDIENTS 🍴YIELDS | 4 SERVES

4 bone-in chicken thighs
2 cups buttermilk (substitute: regular
milk mixed with 1 tablespoon of
vinegar or lemon juice)
1 cup all-purpose flour (substitute:
gluten-free flour blend)
1/2 cup cornstarch

3 tsp garlic powder (divided)
3 tsp onion powder (divided)
2 tsp smoked paprika (divided)
1/2 tsp cayenne pepper (optional for
extra heat)
Salt and pepper to taste
Cooking spray

● DIRECTIONS 🕐 PREP TIME | 15 MIN 🍳 COOK TIME | 20 MIN

1| In a large bowl, combine chicken thighs, buttermilk, 1 tsp garlic powder, 1 tsp onion powder, 1/2 tsp smoked paprika, 1/4 tsp cayenne pepper (if using), and a pinch of salt and pepper. Cover and refrigerate for at least 1 hour, preferably overnight. **2|** Preheat the air fryer to 375°F (190°C). Lightly spray the basket with cooking spray. **3|** Mix flour, cornstarch, remaining 2 tsp garlic powder, 2 tsp onion powder, 1 1/2 tsp smoked paprika, 1/4 tsp cayenne pepper (if using), salt, and pepper. Remove chicken from buttermilk and let excess drip off. Dredge in flour mixture, shaking off excess. **4|** To avoid overcrowding, place coated chicken in the air fryer basket in a single layer. Lightly spray with cooking spray. Cook at 375°F (190°C) for 18-20 minutes, turning halfway, until golden brown and crispy. The internal temperature should reach 165°F (75°C). Let rest a few minutes before serving.

BBQ **CHICKEN DRUMSTICKS**

● INGREDIENTS 🍴YIELDS | 4 SERVES

8 chicken drumsticks
1/2 cup BBQ sauce (substitute: homemade
BBQ sauce)
1 tbsp olive oil
1/2 tsp black pepper

1/2 tsp salt
1 tsp garlic powder
1 tsp onion powder
1 tsp smoked paprika
Cooking spray

● DIRECTIONS 🕐 PREP TIME | 10 MIN 🍳 COOK TIME | 25 MIN

1| Mix olive oil, garlic powder, onion powder, smoked paprika, black pepper, and salt in a large bowl. Add drumsticks and toss to coat. **2|** Preheat the air fryer to 375°F (190°C) and lightly spray the basket with cooking spray. Place drumsticks in a single layer. **3|** Cook at 375°F (190°C) for 20 minutes, turning halfway. Brush with BBQ sauce and cook for 5 minutes, until internal temperature reaches 165°F (74°C) and drumsticks are glazed. **4|** Remove from fryer and let rest for a few minutes before serving.

CRISPY SWEET **AND SOUR CHICKEN NUGGETS**

● INGREDIENTS  YIELDS | 4 SERVES

For the Chicken Nuggets:
1 pound boneless, skinless chicken breasts, cut into 1-inch pieces
1 cup all-purpose flour
1 teaspoon salt
1/2 teaspoon black pepper
1/2 teaspoon garlic powder
1/2 teaspoon onion powder
2 large eggs, beaten
2 cups panko breadcrumbs

Cooking spray
For the Sweet and Sour Sauce:
1/2 cup pineapple juice
1/3 cup rice vinegar
1/3 cup ketchup
1/3 cup brown sugar
1 tablespoon soy sauce
2 teaspoons cornstarch mixed with 2 teaspoons water (for thickening)

● DIRECTIONS ⏱ PREP TIME | 20 MIN 🔲 COOK TIME | 15 MIN

1 | Combine flour, salt, black pepper, garlic powder, and onion powder in a shallow dish. Place beaten eggs in a second dish and panko breadcrumbs in a third. **2 |** Dredge chicken pieces in the flour mixture, shake off excess, dip into beaten eggs, then coat with panko breadcrumbs, pressing gently to adhere. **3 |** Preheat the air fryer to 400°F (200°C) and lightly spray the basket with cooking spray. Arrange coated chicken pieces in a single layer without overlapping. Lightly spray tops with cooking spray. **4 |** Cook at 400°F (200°C) for 10-12 minutes, flipping halfway, until chicken is golden brown and internal temperature reaches 165°F (75°C). **5 |** Mix pineapple juice, rice vinegar, ketchup, brown sugar, and soy sauce in a saucepan over medium heat. Simmer for 2-3 minutes, stirring occasionally. Stir in the cornstarch mixture and cook for 1-2 minutes until sauce thickens. **6 |** Toss the finished chicken nuggets in the sweet and sour sauce. Serve immediately, garnished with chopped green onions or sesame seeds if desired.

MAPLE GLAZED **TURKEY THIGHS**

● INGREDIENTS  YIELDS | 4 SERVES

4 turkey thighs
1/4 cup pure maple syrup
2 tbsp soy sauce (or tamari for gluten-free)
2 tbsp Dijon mustard
2 tbsp olive oil

3 cloves garlic, minced
1 tsp fresh thyme leaves, chopped
1/2 tsp black pepper
1/2 tsp salt
Cooking spray

● DIRECTIONS ⏱ PREP TIME | 15 MIN  COOK TIME | 25 MIN

1 | Whisk together maple syrup, soy sauce, Dijon mustard, olive oil, garlic, thyme, pepper, and salt. Place turkey thighs in a resealable bag or shallow dish, pour marinade over them, and coat them well. Marinate in the refrigerator for at least 1 hour. **2 |** Preheat the air fryer to 375°F (190°C) and lightly spray the basket with cooking spray. Remove the thighs from the marinade and place them in a single layer in the basket. **3 |** Cook at 375°F (190°C) for 25-30 minutes, turning halfway, until golden brown and crispy, with internal temperature at 165°F (75°C). Remove and let rest before serving.

SPICY **BUFFALO CHICKEN TENDERS**

● INGREDIENTS YIELDS | 4 SERVES

1 lb chicken tenders
1 cup all-purpose flour (substitute: gluten-free flour blend)
2 large eggs, beaten
1 cup panko breadcrumbs
1/2 cup hot sauce (such as Frank's RedHot)
1/4 cup melted butter

1 tsp garlic powder
1 tsp onion powder
1/2 tsp smoked paprika
1/4 tsp cayenne pepper (optional for extra heat)
Salt and pepper to taste
Cooking spray

● DIRECTIONS PREP TIME | 10 MIN COOK TIME | 15 MIN

1 | Preheat the air fryer to 400°F (200°C). Lightly spray the air fryer basket with cooking spray. Set up a breading station with three shallow bowls: one with flour, one with beaten eggs, and one with a mixture of panko breadcrumbs, garlic powder, onion powder, smoked paprika, cayenne pepper, salt, and pepper.
2 | Dredge each chicken tender in the flour, shaking off excess. Dip into the beaten eggs, then coat with the panko mixture, pressing lightly to adhere. Place breaded tenders in the air fryer basket in a single layer, avoiding overcrowding. Lightly spray the top with cooking spray.
3 | Cook at 400°F (200°C) for 12-15 minutes, turning halfway through, until golden brown and crispy, with an internal temperature of 165°F (74°C).
4 | While cooking, combine hot sauce and melted butter to prepare the Buffalo sauce.
5 | Remove cooked chicken, toss with Buffalo sauce, and serve immediately.

LEMON HERB **CHICKEN BREASTS**

● INGREDIENTS YIELDS | 4 SERVES

4 boneless, skinless chicken breasts
1/4 cup olive oil
1/4 cup lemon juice (freshly squeezed)
1 tbsp lemon zest
2 cloves garlic, minced

1 tsp dried oregano
1 tsp dried thyme
1 tsp dried rosemary
Salt and pepper to taste
Cooking spray

● DIRECTIONS PREP TIME | 10 MIN COOK TIME | 15 MIN

1 | Preheat the air fryer to 375°F (190°C) and lightly spray the basket with cooking spray.
2 | Mix olive oil, lemon juice, zest, garlic, oregano, thyme, rosemary, salt, and pepper in a bowl.
3 | Pat chicken breasts dry, brush with the lemon herb mixture, and place in the air fryer basket in a single layer.
4 | Cook at 375°F (190°C) for 12-15 minutes, turning halfway, until internal temperature reaches 165°F (74°C).
5 | Remove and let rest for a few minutes before serving.

FLAVORFUL CHICKEN WINGS

● INGREDIENTS  YIELDS | 4 SERVES

2 pounds of chicken wings, separated at the joints and tips, were removed
2 tablespoons olive oil
For the Honey Garlic Marinade:
1/4 cup honey
3 cloves garlic, minced
2 tablespoons soy sauce
1 tablespoon apple cider vinegar
1 teaspoon salt

1/2 teaspoon black pepper
For the Italian Herb Marinade:
1/4 cup olive oil
2 tablespoons lemon juice
3 cloves garlic, minced
1 tablespoon dried oregano
1 tablespoon dried basil
1 teaspoon salt
1/2 teaspoon black pepper

● DIRECTIONS ⏱ PREP TIME | 15 MIN 🍳 COOK TIME | 25 MIN

1 | Prepare the marinades in two bowls. For the honey garlic marinade, mix honey, garlic, soy sauce, vinegar, salt, and pepper. For the Italian Herb Marinade, mix olive oil, lemon juice, garlic, oregano, basil, salt, and pepper. Divide the chicken wings into two portions, coat them with their respective marinades, cover, and refrigerate for at least 1 hour or overnight. **2 |** Preheat the air fryer to 375°F (190°C) and lightly spray the basket with cooking spray. Arrange marinated wings in a single layer without overlapping. Cook in batches if needed. **3 |** Cook at 375°F (190°C) for 25 minutes, flipping halfway, until crispy and the internal temperature reaches 165°F (75°C).
4 | Remove wings from the air fryer and let cool slightly before serving.

QUICK ENCHILADA DELIGHT

● INGREDIENTS  YIELDS | 4 SERVES

2 cups cooked, shredded chicken
1 cup enchilada sauce, divided
1 cup shredded cheddar cheese
1/2 cup shredded Monterey Jack cheese
1/4 cup diced onions

1/4 cup diced bell peppers
8 small flour tortillas
Cooking spray
Fresh cilantro and sliced jalapeños for garnish (optional)

● DIRECTIONS ⏱ PREP TIME | 15 MIN 🍳 COOK TIME | 20 MIN

1 | Mix the shredded chicken, 1/2 cup of enchilada sauce, diced onions, and bell peppers in a large bowl. **2 |** Lay out the flour tortillas and evenly distribute the chicken mixture onto each one. Sprinkle with a small amount of shredded cheddar and Monterey Jack cheese. **3 |** Roll up each tortilla tightly and place them seam-side down in an air fryer-safe baking dish that fits your air fryer. **4 |** Lightly spray the rolled enchiladas with cooking spray. Preheat the air fryer to 350°F (175°C) for about 5 minutes. **5 |** Place the baking dish with the enchiladas in the preheated air fryer. Cook at 350°F (175°C) for 10 minutes. **6 |** Carefully remove the dish and pour the remaining enchilada sauce over the enchiladas. Sprinkle with the remaining shredded cheese. **7 |** Return the dish to the air fryer and cook for 10 minutes or until the cheese melts and becomes bubbly. **8 |** Remove from the air fryer and let cool slightly before serving. Garnish with fresh cilantro and sliced jalapeños if desired.

PARMESAN CRUSTED **CHICKEN THIGHS**

● **INGREDIENTS** 🪙 YIELDS | 4 SERVES

4 bone-in, skin-on chicken thighs
1/2 cup grated Parmesan cheese
1/2 cup panko breadcrumbs
(substitute: regular breadcrumbs)
1 tsp garlic powder
1 tsp onion powder

4 bone-in, skin-on chicken thighs
1/2 cup grated Parmesan cheese
1/2 cup panko breadcrumbs
(substitute: regular breadcrumbs)
1 tsp garlic powder
1 tsp onion powder

● **DIRECTIONS** ⏱ PREP TIME | 15 MIN 🍳 COOK TIME | 25 MIN

1 | In a bowl, mix the Parmesan, panko, garlic powder, onion powder, oregano, thyme, salt, and pepper. In another bowl, beat the eggs.
2 | Pat chicken thighs dry. Dip each thigh in the beaten eggs, then coat with the Parmesan mixture, pressing lightly to adhere.
3 | Preheat the air fryer to 375°F (190°C) and lightly spray the basket with cooking spray. Place coated thighs in a single layer.
4 | Cook at 375°F (190°C) for 18-20 minutes, turning halfway, until golden brown and crispy. Internal temperature should reach 165°F (74°C).
5 | Remove from fryer and let rest for a few minutes before serving.

ITALIAN **CHICKEN ROLLS**

● **INGREDIENTS** 🪙 YIELDS | 4 SERVES

4 boneless, skinless chicken breasts
1/2 cup sun-dried tomatoes (packed
in oil), chopped
1/2 cup fresh basil leaves, chopped
1 cup shredded mozzarella cheese
1/4 cup grated Parmesan cheese

1 tsp Italian seasoning
2 cloves garlic, minced
Salt and pepper to taste
2 tbsp olive oil
Cooking spray
Marinara sauce for serving

● **DIRECTIONS** ⏱ PREP TIME | 20 MIN 🍳 COOK TIME | 25 MIN

1 | Preheat the air fryer to 375°F (190°C) and lightly spray the basket with cooking spray. Pound chicken breasts to 1/4-inch thickness using a meat mallet or rolling pin.
2 | Mix sun-dried tomatoes, basil, mozzarella, Parmesan, garlic, Italian seasoning, salt, and pepper in a bowl.
3 | Lay chicken breasts flat. Spoon an equal amount of filling onto each, roll up tightly, and secure with toothpicks. Brush the outside of each roll with olive oil.
4 | Place chicken rolls in a single layer in the air fryer basket to avoid overcrowding. Cook at 375°F (190°C) for 20-25 minutes, turning halfway, until golden brown and internal temperature reaches 165°F (75°C).
5 | Remove from the fryer, rest for a few minutes, and remove toothpicks. Serve with marinara sauce.

TERIYAKI **MEAT SKEWERS**

 **INGREDIENTS** **YIELDS | 4 SERVES**

1 pound boneless, skinless chicken
breasts or thighs cut into 1-inch pieces
1 pound boneless, skinless turkey
breasts or thighs cut into 1-inch pieces
1 red bell pepper, cut into 1-inch
pieces
1 yellow bell pepper, cut into 1-inch
pieces
1 red onion, cut into 1-inch pieces
Wooden or metal skewers (if using
wooden skewers, soak them in water
for 30 minutes)

For the Teriyaki Marinade:
1/2 cup soy sauce
1/4 cup brown sugar
1/4 cup mirin (sweet rice wine)
2 tablespoons honey
2 tablespoons rice vinegar
2 cloves garlic, minced
1 tablespoon grated fresh ginger
1 tablespoon sesame oil
1 teaspoon cornstarch (optional for
thickening)

DIRECTIONS **PREP TIME | 20 MIN** **COOK TIME | 12 MIN**

1 | In a bowl, mix soy sauce, brown sugar, mirin, honey, rice vinegar, garlic, ginger, and sesame oil. Dissolve cornstarch in water and add it for a thicker marinade. **2 |** Divide the marinade into two portions. Place chicken in one and turkey in the other. Coat well, cover, and refrigerate for at least 1 hour. **3 |** Preheat the air fryer to 375°F (190°C)—thread chicken, turkey, bell peppers, and onion onto skewers, alternating pieces. **4 |** Lightly spray the air fryer basket with cooking spray. Arrange the skewers in a single layer. **5 |** Cook at 375°F (190°C) for 10-12 minutes, turning halfway, until the meat is cooked and veggies are lightly charred. The internal temperature should reach 165°F (75°C). **6 |** Remove skewers from the air fryer and let cool slightly before serving.

HERB-CRUSTED **TURKEY BREAST**

 **INGREDIENTS** **YIELDS | 4 SERVES**

1 lb boneless, skinless turkey breast
2 tbsp olive oil
3 cloves garlic, minced
1 tbsp fresh rosemary, finely chopped
1 tbsp fresh thyme, finely chopped
1 tbsp fresh parsley, finely chopped

1 tsp dried oregano
1/2 tsp salt
1/2 tsp black pepper
Cooking spray
Lemon wedges (optional for serving)

DIRECTIONS **PREP TIME | 15 MIN** **COOK TIME | 25 MIN**

1 | Mix olive oil, garlic, rosemary, thyme, parsley, oregano, salt, and pepper. Pat turkey breast dry and rub with herb mixture. **2 |** Marinating the turkey is a breeze. Simply place it in a resealable bag or covered dish in the fridge for 1-2 hours. **3 |** Preheat the air fryer to 375°F (190°C). Lightly spray the basket with cooking spray. Place the turkey in a single layer in the basket. **4 |** Cook at 375°F (190°C) for 20-25 minutes, turning halfway, until golden brown and crispy and the internal temperature reaches 165°F (75°C). **5 |** Let the turkey rest for a few minutes before slicing. Serve with lemon wedges if desired.

THAI PEANUT **CHICKEN SKEWERS**

● INGREDIENTS YIELDS | 4 SERVES

1 lb boneless, skinless chicken breasts
cut into bite-sized pieces
1/4 cup creamy peanut butter
2 tbsp soy sauce
1 tbsp lime juice (freshly squeezed)
1 tbsp honey
1 tbsp sesame oil
2 cloves garlic, minced
1 tsp ginger, minced

1/2 tsp crushed red pepper flakes
(optional for extra heat)
1/4 cup chopped fresh cilantro
(optional, for garnish)
Chopped peanuts (optional, for
garnish)
Lime wedges (optional for serving)
Cooking spray

● DIRECTIONS PREP TIME | 20 MIN COOK TIME | 30 MIN

1 | In a large bowl, whisk together peanut butter, soy sauce, lime juice, honey, sesame oil, garlic, ginger, and crushed red pepper flakes (if using). Add chicken pieces and toss to coat—Marinate in the refrigerator for at least 30 minutes. **2 |** Soak wooden skewers in water for at least 10 minutes while marinating. **3 |** Preheat the air fryer to 375°F (190°C). Lightly spray the basket with cooking spray. **4 |** Thread marinated chicken pieces onto skewers. Place skewers in a single layer in the air fryer basket. **5 |** Cook at 375°F (190°C) for 10-12 minutes, turning halfway, until the chicken reaches an internal temperature of 165°F (75°C). Remove and let rest. **6 |** Garnish with chopped fresh cilantro and peanuts. Serve with lime wedges.

CLASSIC **TURKEY MEATBALLS**

● INGREDIENTS YIELDS | 4 SERVES

1 lb ground turkey
1/2 cup breadcrumbs
1/4 cup grated Parmesan cheese
1/4 cup finely chopped onion
2 cloves garlic, minced
1 large egg
2 tbsp milk
2 tbsp fresh parsley, chopped

1 tsp dried oregano
1 tsp dried basil
1/2 tsp salt
1/2 tsp black pepper
Cooking spray
Marinara sauce (optional for serving)
Cooked pasta (optional for serving)

● DIRECTIONS PREP TIME | 15 MIN COOK TIME | 15 MIN

1 | Combine ground turkey, breadcrumbs, Parmesan cheese, onion, garlic, egg, milk, parsley, oregano, basil, salt, and black pepper in a large bowl. Mix well until all ingredients are evenly incorporated. **2 |** Form the mixture into meatballs about 1 inch in diameter. **3 |** Preheat the air fryer to 375°F (190°C) and lightly spray the basket with cooking spray. Place the meatballs in a single layer without overcrowding. **4 |** Cook at 375°F (190°C) for 12-15 minutes, shaking the basket halfway, until golden brown and cooked through. The internal temperature should reach 165°F (75°C). **5 |** Remove the meatballs from the fryer and let them rest for a few minutes before serving. If desired, serve with marinara sauce and cooked pasta.

SPICED ORANGE **GLAZED DUCK LEGS**

● **INGREDIENTS** 🥞 **YIELDS** | 4 SERVES

4 duck legs
1/2 cup fresh orange juice
1/4 cup soy sauce (or tamari for
gluten-free)
2 tbsp honey
2 tbsp hoisin sauce
1 tbsp rice vinegar
1 tbsp olive oil
2 cloves garlic, minced

1 tsp grated fresh ginger
1/2 tsp five-spice powder
1/4 tsp red pepper flakes (optional,
for heat)
Salt and pepper to taste
Cooking spray
Fresh cilantro, chopped (optional, for
garnish)

● **DIRECTIONS** ⏱ PREP TIME | 15 MIN 🍳 COOK TIME | 35 MIN

1 | Mix orange juice, soy sauce, honey, hoisin sauce, rice vinegar, olive oil, garlic, ginger, five-spice powder, red pepper flakes (if using), salt, and pepper. Place duck legs in a resealable bag or dish, pour the marinade, and coat well. Marinate in refrigerator for at least 1 hour. **2 |** Preheat the air fryer to 375°F (190°C) and lightly spray the basket with cooking spray. Remove the duck legs from the marinade and place them in a single layer in the basket. **3 |** Cook at 375°F (190°C) for 35-40 minutes, turning halfway, until golden brown and crispy and the internal temperature reaches 165°F (75°C). While cooking, transfer the remaining marinade to a saucepan, boil over medium-high heat, and simmer for 5-7 minutes until thickened. **4 |** Remove duck legs from the fryer and let them rest for a few minutes. Drizzle thickened sauce over the duck legs and garnish with fresh cilantro, if desired.

GREEK SPINACH **AND FETA CHICKEN ROLLS**

● **INGREDIENTS** 🥞 **YIELDS** | 4 SERVES

4 boneless, skinless chicken breasts
1 cup fresh spinach, chopped
1/2 cup crumbled feta cheese
1/4 cup sun-dried tomatoes, chopped
2 cloves garlic, minced
1 tbsp olive oil
1 tsp dried oregano

1 tsp dried basil
1/2 tsp black pepper
Salt to taste
Cooking spray
Lemon wedges (optional for serving)
Fresh parsley, chopped (optional, for
garnish)

● **DIRECTIONS** ⏱ PREP TIME | 20 MIN 🍳 COOK TIME | 20 MIN

1 | Mix spinach, feta, sun-dried tomatoes, garlic, olive oil, oregano, basil, black pepper, and salt in a bowl. **2 |** Pound chicken breasts to 1/4-inch thickness using a meat mallet or rolling pin. Spread the spinach and feta mixture evenly over each chicken breast. **3 |** Roll up each chicken breast tightly and secure it with toothpicks. **4 |** Preheat the air fryer to 375°F (190°C) and lightly spray the basket with cooking spray. Place chicken rolls in a single layer without overcrowding. **5 |** Cook at 375°F (190°C) for 18-20 minutes, turning halfway, until golden brown and internal temperature reaches 165°F (75°C). **6 |** Remove from the fryer, rest for a few minutes, and remove toothpicks. Garnish with fresh parsley and serve with lemon wedges if desired.

HOISIN GLAZED **DUCK WINGS**

● **INGREDIENTS** 🥟 YIELDS | 4 SERVES

2 lbs duck wings
1/2 cup hoisin sauce
1/4 cup soy sauce (or tamari for gluten-free)
2 tbsp honey
2 tbsp rice vinegar
2 cloves garlic, minced
1 tsp grated fresh ginger

1/2 tsp five-spice powder
1/4 tsp red pepper flakes (optional, for heat)
1 tbsp sesame oil
Cooking spray
Sesame seeds (optional, for garnish)
Chopped green onions (optional, for garnish)

● **DIRECTIONS** ⏱ PREP TIME | 15 MIN 🍳 COOK TIME | 25 MIN

1 | Mix hoisin sauce, soy sauce, honey, rice vinegar, garlic, ginger, five-spice powder, red pepper flakes (if using), and sesame oil. Place duck wings in a bag or dish, pour the marinade over them, and coat them well. Marinate in the fridge for at least 1 hour. **2 |** Preheat the air fryer to 375°F (190°C) and lightly spray the basket with cooking spray. Remove the wings from the marinade and place them in a single layer in the basket. **3 |** Cook at 375°F (190°C) for 20-25 minutes, turning halfway, until golden brown and crispy. Boil the remaining marinade, then simmer for 5-7 minutes until thickened. **4 |** Let the wings rest for a few minutes. Drizzle thickened sauce over wings and garnish with sesame seeds and green onions, if desired.

LEMON **ROSEMARY HEN**

● **INGREDIENTS** 🥟 YIELDS | 4 SERVES

2 Cornish game hens, split in half
2 tbsp olive oil
2 lemons (1 sliced, 1 juiced)
4 cloves garlic, minced
2 tbsp fresh rosemary, chopped

1 tbsp fresh thyme, chopped
1 tsp salt
1/2 tsp black pepper
Cooking spray
Fresh parsley, chopped (optional, for garnish)

● **DIRECTIONS** ⏱ PREP TIME | 15 MIN 🍳 COOK TIME | 40 MIN

1 | Mix olive oil, juice of 1 lemon, garlic, rosemary, thyme, salt, and pepper in a bowl. Pat hens dry with paper towels and rub with herb mixture—Marinate in a resealable bag or dish in the refrigerator for at least 1 hour. **2 |** Preheat the air fryer to 375°F (190°C) and lightly spray the basket with cooking spray. Place lemon slices in the basket. Remove hens from marinade and place on lemon slices skin side up. **3 |** Cook at 375°F (190°C) for 40-45 minutes, turning halfway, until skin is golden brown and crispy and internal temperature reaches 165°F (75°C). **4 |** Remove the hens from the fryer and let them rest for a few minutes. If desired, garnish with parsley and additional lemon wedges.

HONEY SOY **DUCK THIGHS**

● INGREDIENTS 🥞 YIELDS | 4 SERVES

4 duck thighs
1/4 cup soy sauce (or tamari for
gluten-free)
1/4 cup honey
2 tbsp rice vinegar
2 tbsp sesame oil
2 cloves garlic, minced

1 tsp grated fresh ginger
1/2 tsp black pepper
1/4 tsp red pepper flakes (optional,
for heat)
Cooking spray
Sesame seeds (optional, for garnish)
Chopped green onions (optional, for
garnish)

● DIRECTIONS ⏱ PREP TIME | 15 MIN 🍳 COOK TIME | 25 MIN

1 | Mix soy sauce, honey, rice vinegar, sesame oil, garlic, ginger, black pepper, and red flakes (if used). Place duck thighs in a bag or dish, pour marinade over them, and coat them well. Marinate in the fridge for at least 1 hour.

2 | Preheat the air fryer to 375°F (190°C) and lightly spray the basket with cooking spray. Remove thighs from the marinade and place in a single layer in the basket.

3 | Cook at 375°F (190°C) for 25-30 minutes, turning halfway, until golden brown and crispy and internal temperature reaches 165°F (75°C). While cooking, boil the remaining marinade over medium-high heat, then simmer for 5-7 minutes until thickened.

4 | Remove thighs from the fryer and let rest for a few minutes. Drizzle thickened sauce over thighs and garnish with sesame seeds and green onions, if desired.

SAVORY **GARLIC QUAIL**

● INGREDIENTS 🥞 YIELDS | 4 SERVES

4 quails, cleaned and split in half
3 tbsp olive oil
4 cloves garlic, minced
2 tbsp fresh rosemary, chopped
2 tbsp fresh thyme, chopped

2 tbsp fresh parsley, chopped
1 tsp salt
1/2 tsp black pepper
Cooking spray
Lemon wedges (optional for serving)

● DIRECTIONS ⏱ PREP TIME | 15 MIN 🍳 COOK TIME | 25 MIN

1 | Mix olive oil, garlic, rosemary, thyme, parsley, salt, and pepper in a bowl. Pat quails dry with paper towels and rub with the herb mixture. Marinate in a resealable bag or dish in the refrigerator for at least 1 hour.

2 | Preheat the air fryer to 375°F (190°C) and lightly spray the basket with cooking spray. Remove the quails from the marinade and place them skin-side up in a single layer in the basket.

3 | Cook at 375°F (190°C) for 20-25 minutes, turning halfway, until the skin is golden brown and crispy and the internal temperature reaches 165°F (75°C).

4 | Remove quails from the fryer and let rest for a few minutes. Serve with lemon wedges if desired.

DUCK À L'ORANGE

● **INGREDIENTS** 🍽 **YIELDS** | 4 SERVES

4 duck breasts
1/2 cup fresh orange juice
1/4 cup chicken broth
1/4 cup orange marmalade
2 tbsp soy sauce
2 tbsp honey
1 tbsp balsamic vinegar
2 cloves garlic, minced

1 tsp grated fresh ginger
Zest of 1 orange
Salt and pepper to taste
Cooking spray
Orange slices (optional, for garnish)
Fresh parsley, chopped (optional, for garnish)

● **DIRECTIONS** ⏱ **PREP TIME** | 20 MIN 🍳 **COOK TIME** | 35 MIN

1 |Mix a bowl of orange juice, chicken broth, orange marmalade, soy sauce, honey, balsamic vinegar, garlic, ginger, and orange zest. Set aside. **2** |Pat duck breasts dry with paper towels. Score skin in a crosshatch pattern, being careful not to cut into meat. Season both sides with salt and pepper. **3** |Preheat the air fryer to 375°F (190°C). Lightly spray the basket with cooking spray. Place the duck breasts skin-side down in the basket without overcrowding. **4** | Cook at 375°F (190°C) for 20 minutes. Turn duck breasts and cook for another 10-15 minutes until the internal temperature reaches 165°F (75°C) and the skin is crispy. **5** | While the duck is cooking, prepare the orange sauce. In a saucepan, bring the orange juice mixture to a boil over medium-high heat. Reduce heat and simmer for 10 minutes until the sauce thickens slightly. **6** | Remove duck breasts from the fryer and let them rest for a few minutes before slicing. Serve with orange sauce drizzled over the top. Garnish with orange slices and chopped parsley if desired.

CHINESE FIVE SPICE CHICKEN WINGS

● **INGREDIENTS** 🍽 **YIELDS** | 4 SERVES

2 lbs chicken wings
2 tbsp soy sauce (or tamari for gluten-free)
1 tbsp hoisin sauce
1 tbsp honey
1 tbsp rice vinegar
2 cloves garlic, minced
1 tsp grated fresh ginger

1 tsp Chinese five-spice powder
1/2 tsp salt
1/2 tsp black pepper
Cooking spray
Sesame seeds (optional, for garnish)
Chopped green onions (optional, for garnish)

● **DIRECTIONS** ⏱ **PREP TIME** | 15 MIN 🍳 **COOK TIME** | 25 MIN

1 | Mix a large bowl of soy sauce, hoisin sauce, honey, rice vinegar, garlic, ginger, Chinese five-spice powder, salt, and black pepper. Add chicken wings and toss to coat—Marinate in the refrigerator for at least 1 hour. **2** | Preheat the air fryer to 375°F (190°C) and lightly spray the basket with cooking spray. Remove the wings from the marinade, allowing the excess to drip off. Place the wings in a single layer in the basket. **3** | Cook at 375°F (190°C) for 20-25 minutes, turning halfway, until wings are golden brown and crispy and internal temperature reaches 165°F (75°C). **4** | Remove the wings from the fryer and let them rest for a few minutes before serving. If desired, garnish with sesame seeds and chopped green onions.

MEXICAN CHICKEN FAJITAS

● INGREDIENTS 🍳 YIELDS | 4 SERVES

1 lb boneless, skinless chicken breasts
cut into thin strips
1 red bell pepper, sliced
1 green bell pepper, sliced
1 yellow bell pepper, sliced
1 tsp smoked paprika
1 tsp garlic powder
1 tsp onion powder
1/2 tsp dried oregano
1/2 tsp salt
1/2 tsp black pepper

1 large onion, sliced
2 tbsp olive oil
2 tsp chili powder
1 tsp ground cumin
Juice of 1 lime
Cooking spray
Warm tortillas (for serving)
Fresh cilantro, chopped (optional, for garnish)
Salsa, sour cream, and guacamole (optional for serving)

● DIRECTIONS ⏱ PREP TIME | 20 MIN 🍳 COOK TIME | 18 MIN

1 | In a large bowl, mix olive oil, chili powder, cumin, smoked paprika, garlic powder, onion powder, oregano, salt, black pepper, and lime juice. Add chicken strips, bell peppers, and onion slices, tossing to coat evenly. **2 |** Preheat the air fryer to 375°F (190°C) and lightly spray the basket with cooking spray. Place the marinated chicken, peppers, and onions in a single layer in the basket. **3 |** Cook at 375°F (190°C) for 15-18 minutes, shaking the basket or stirring halfway through until the chicken is cooked and the vegetables are tender and lightly charred. **4 |** Remove fajitas from the fryer. Serve with warm tortillas and garnish with chopped cilantro if desired. Offer salsa, sour cream, and guacamole on the side.

SOUTHERN FRIED QUAIL

● INGREDIENTS 🍳 YIELDS | 4 SERVES

4 quails, cleaned and split in half
1 cup buttermilk
1 tsp hot sauce (optional)
1 cup all-purpose flour
1 cup cornmeal
1 tsp paprika

1 tsp garlic powder
1 tsp onion powder
1/2 tsp cayenne pepper (optional)
1 tsp salt
1/2 tsp black pepper
Cooking spray

● DIRECTIONS ⏱ PREP TIME | 20 MIN 🍳 COOK TIME | 20 MIN

1 | Mix buttermilk and hot sauce (if used) in a bowl. Place quails in the buttermilk mixture, ensuring they are fully submerged—Marinate in the refrigerator for at least 1 hour. **2 |** In another bowl, mix flour, cornmeal, paprika, garlic powder, onion powder, cayenne pepper (if using), salt, and black pepper. **3 |** Remove the quails from the buttermilk, allowing the excess to drip off. Dredge each quail in the flour mixture, pressing lightly to adhere.
4 | Preheat the air fryer to 375°F (190°C) and lightly spray the basket with cooking spray. Place the breaded quails in a single layer in the basket. **5 |** Lightly spray the tops of the quails with cooking spray. Cook at 375°F (190°C) for 15-20 minutes, turning halfway, until golden brown and crispy and the internal temperature reaches 165°F (75°C). **6 |** Remove quails from the fryer and let rest a few minutes before serving.

ARGENTINE CHICKEN EMPANADAS

● INGREDIENTS   YIELDS | 4 SERVES

For the Dough:
2 1/2 cups all-purpose flour
1/2 cup unsalted butter, chilled and cut into small pieces
1 tsp salt
1/2 cup cold water
For Assembly:
1 large egg, beaten (for egg wash)
Cooking spray
For the Filling:
1 lb boneless, skinless chicken breasts, cooked and shredded

1 small onion, finely chopped
1 red bell pepper, finely chopped
2 cloves garlic, minced
2 tbsp olive oil
1/2 cup green olives, sliced
1/4 cup raisins (optional)
1 tsp ground cumin
1 tsp smoked paprika
1/2 tsp ground chili powder
Salt and pepper to taste
1/4 cup fresh parsley, chopped
1 hard-boiled egg, chopped (optional)

● DIRECTIONS   PREP TIME | 30 MIN   COOK TIME | 18 MIN

1 | Mix flour and salt in a large bowl. Add chilled butter and mix until coarse crumbs form. Gradually add cold water, mixing until dough forms. Knead briefly until smooth, wrap in plastic and refrigerate for 30 minutes. **2 |** Heat olive oil in a skillet over medium heat. Sauté onion, red bell pepper, and garlic until soft. Add shredded chicken, olives, raisins (if using), cumin, paprika, chili powder, salt, and pepper. Cook until combined and heated through. Remove from heat, stir in parsley and hard-boiled egg (if using), and let cool. **3 |** Preheat the air fryer to 375°F (190°C) and lightly spray the basket with cooking spray. Roll out chilled dough on a floured surface to 1/8-inch thickness. Cut out circles (4-6 inches). **4 |** Place a spoonful of filling in the center of each dough circle. Fold over the filling and seal the edges. Crimp with a fork. Brush with beaten egg. **5 |** Place empanadas in a single layer in the air fryer basket. Cook at 375°F (190°C) for 15-18 minutes, turning halfway, until golden brown and crispy. Let cool slightly before serving.

CRUNCHY GARLIC CHICKEN HEARTS

● INGREDIENTS   YIELDS | 4 SERVES

1 lb chicken hearts
2 tbsp olive oil
2 cloves garlic, minced
1/2 tsp salt
1/2 tsp black pepper

1/2 tsp paprika
1/2 tsp onion powder
1/4 tsp cayenne pepper (optional)
1/2 cup panko breadcrumbs
Cooking spray

● DIRECTIONS   PREP TIME | 15 MIN   COOK TIME | 15 MIN

1 | Clean chicken hearts by removing excess fat or membranes and rinsing them under cold water. **2 |** In a large bowl, combine olive oil, garlic, salt, black pepper, paprika, onion powder, and cayenne pepper (if using). Add chicken hearts and toss to coat evenly. **3 |** Preheat the air fryer to 375°F (190°C) and lightly spray the basket with cooking spray. Place panko breadcrumbs in a shallow bowl. Dredge each seasoned chicken heart in breadcrumbs, pressing lightly to adhere.
4 | Arrange coated chicken hearts in a single layer in the basket. Lightly spray with cooking spray.
5 | Cook at 375°F (190°C) for 12-15 minutes, turning halfway, until golden brown and crispy. Let rest a few minutes before serving.

THAI CHICKEN SATAY

● INGREDIENTS  YIELDS | 4 SERVES

For the Chicken Satay:
1 lb boneless, skinless chicken breasts cut into thin strips
2 tbsp soy sauce (or tamari for gluten-free)
2 tbsp fish sauce
2 tbsp coconut milk
2 cloves garlic, minced
1 tsp grated fresh ginger
1 tsp ground coriander
1 tsp ground turmeric
1/2 tsp cumin
1/2 tsp chili powder
1 tbsp brown sugar
1 tbsp vegetable oil

Wooden skewers soaked in water for at least 30 minutes
For the Peanut Sauce:
1/2 cup creamy peanut butter
2 tbsp soy sauce
1 tbsp fish sauce
1 tbsp lime juice (freshly squeezed)
1 tbsp brown sugar
1 tsp red curry paste (optional, for heat)
1/2 cup coconut milk
Water (to thin the sauce, if necessary)
For Garnish:
Fresh cilantro, chopped
Lime wedges

● DIRECTIONS  PREP TIME | 20 MIN  COOK TIME | 15 MIN

1 | In a bowl, combine soy sauce, fish sauce, coconut milk, garlic, ginger, coriander, turmeric, cumin, chili powder, brown sugar, and vegetable oil. Add chicken strips and mix to coat. Marinate in refrigerator for at least 1 hour. **2 |** Prepare the peanut sauce: combine peanut butter, soy sauce, fish sauce, lime juice, brown sugar, red curry paste (if using), and coconut milk in a saucepan. Cook over medium heat, stirring until smooth. Add water if needed to reach the desired consistency. Set aside. **3 |** Preheat the air fryer to 375°F (190°C) and lightly spray the basket with cooking spray. Thread marinated chicken strips onto soaked skewers and place them in a single layer in the basket. **4 |** Cook at 375°F (190°C) for 12-15 minutes, turning halfway, until chicken reaches an internal temperature of 165°F (75°C). Remove from fryer and let rest a few minutes before serving. **5 |** Serve chicken satay with peanut sauce, garnished with cilantro and lime wedges.

TERIYAKI CHICKEN JERKY

If your air fryer model has a dehydration function, set it to dehydrating.

● INGREDIENTS YIELDS | 4 SERVES

1 lb chicken breasts, thinly sliced into strips
1/4 cup soy sauce
2 tbsp teriyaki sauce
1 tbsp brown sugar

1 clove garlic, minced
1 tsp ginger, grated
1/2 tsp black pepper

● DIRECTIONS  PREP TIME | 15 MIN DEHYDRATING TIME | 4-5 HOURS

1 | Mix a large bowl of soy sauce, teriyaki sauce, brown sugar, garlic, ginger, and black pepper. Add chicken strips and toss to coat. Cover and refrigerate for 2-4 hours. **2 |** Remove chicken strips from the marinade and pat dry with paper towels. Arrange strips in a single layer in the air fryer basket, avoiding overlap. **3 |** Dehydrate at 160°F (71°C) for 1 hour, then reduce temperature to 130-160°F (55-69°C) and continue dehydrating for 3-4 hours until dry and chewy. **4 |** Excellent jerky entirely before storing in an airtight container.

SPICY CHICKEN LIVER BITES

● INGREDIENTS   YIELDS | 4 SERVES

1 lb chicken livers, cleaned and
trimmed
2 tbsp olive oil
1 tbsp hot sauce (adjust to taste)
2 cloves garlic, minced
1 tsp paprika
1/2 tsp cayenne pepper (optional, for
extra heat)

1/2 tsp onion powder
1/2 tsp black pepper
1/2 tsp salt
1/2 cup all-purpose flour
Cooking spray
Fresh parsley, chopped (optional, for
garnish)

● DIRECTIONS   PREP TIME | 15 MIN   COOK TIME | 15 MIN

1 | Clean chicken livers by removing excess fat and membranes, rinsing them under cold water, and patting them dry with paper towels. Pierce each liver with a fork or toothpick to allow steam to escape during cooking. **2 |** In a large bowl, combine olive oil, hot sauce, garlic, paprika, cayenne pepper (if using), onion powder, black pepper, and salt. Add chicken livers and toss to coat. **3 |** Place flour in a shallow bowl. Dredge each marinated chicken liver in flour, shaking off excess. **4 |** Preheat the air fryer to 375°F (190°C) and lightly spray the basket with cooking spray. Arrange coated livers in a single layer, avoiding overcrowding. Lightly spray with cooking spray. **5 |** Cook at 375°F (190°C) for 12-15 minutes, turning halfway, until golden brown and crispy. Let rest a few minutes before serving. **6 |** Garnish with chopped parsley if desired.

BBQ CHICKEN HEART SKEWERS

● INGREDIENTS   YIELDS | 4 SERVES

1 lb chicken hearts, cleaned and
trimmed
1/2 cup BBQ sauce
2 tbsp olive oil
2 cloves garlic, minced
1 tsp smoked paprika
1/2 tsp black pepper

1/2 tsp salt
Wooden skewers soaked in water for
at least 30 minutes
Cooking spray
Fresh cilantro, chopped (optional, for
garnish)
Lime wedges (optional for serving)

● DIRECTIONS   PREP TIME | 20 MIN   COOK TIME | 15 MIN

1 | Clean chicken hearts by removing excess fat and membranes, rinse them under cold water and pat them dry with paper towels. **2 |** Combine BBQ sauce, olive oil, garlic, smoked paprika, black pepper, and salt in a large bowl. Add chicken hearts and toss to coat evenly—Marinate in the refrigerator for at least 1 hour. **3 |** Preheat the air fryer to 375°F (190°C) and lightly spray the basket with cooking spray. Thread the marinated chicken hearts onto soaked wooden skewers. **4 |** Arrange skewers in a single layer in the basket, avoiding overcrowding. Lightly spray with cooking spray. **5 |** Cook at 375°F (190°C) for 12-15 minutes, turning halfway, until chicken hearts are cooked and lightly charred. Let rest a few minutes before serving. **6 |** Garnish with chopped cilantro and serve with lime wedges if desired.

CHAPTER 4

JUICY MEAT DISHES

MOUTHWATERING RIBEYE STEAK

● INGREDIENTS 📚 YIELDS | 4 SERVES

1 ribeye steak (approximately 1-1.5 inches thick)
2 tablespoons olive oil
2 cloves garlic, minced

1 tablespoon fresh rosemary, chopped
1 tablespoon fresh thyme, chopped
Salt and pepper to taste

● DIRECTIONS ⏱ PREP TIME | 10 MIN 🍳 COOK TIME | 12 MIN

1 | Remove steak from the refrigerator 30 minutes before cooking. Pat dry with a paper towel.
2 | Combine olive oil, garlic, rosemary, and thyme. Rub the mixture on both sides of the steak, then season with salt and pepper. Marinate for 30 minutes.
3 | Preheat the air fryer to 400°F (200°C). Place the steak in the basket flat and without overlapping.
4 | Cook for 10-12 minutes for medium-rare, flipping halfway through. Check internal temperature (130°F/54°C).
5 | Let the steak rest for 5-7 minutes. Slice thinly against the grain and serve.

GARLIC CRUSTED TENDERLOIN

● INGREDIENTS 📚 YIELDS | 4 SERVES

1 beef tenderloin (about 2 pounds)
3 tablespoons olive oil
2 tablespoons fresh thyme, chopped
1 teaspoon salt

4 cloves garlic, minced
2 tablespoons fresh rosemary, chopped
1 teaspoon black pepper

● DIRECTIONS ⏱ PREP TIME | 15 MIN 🍳 COOK TIME | 30 MIN

1 | Mix olive oil, garlic, rosemary, thyme, salt, and pepper. Rub the tenderloin with the mixture and marinate for 30 minutes.
2 | Preheat the air fryer to 375°F (190°C). Place the tenderloin in the basket.
3 | Cook for 25-30 minutes, turning halfway, until the internal temperature reaches 135°F (57°C) for medium-rare.
4 | Let the tenderloin rest for 10-15 minutes before slicing.
5 | Slice into medallions and serve.

QUICK & SAVORY **MEATLOAF**

● **INGREDIENTS** 🍽️ YIELDS | 4 SERVES

1 lb ground beef
1/2 lb ground pork
1 small onion, finely chopped
2 cloves garlic, minced
1/2 cup breadcrumbs
1/4 cup milk

1 egg, beaten
2 tablespoons ketchup
1 tablespoon Worcestershire sauce
1 teaspoon salt
1/2 teaspoon black pepper

● **DIRECTIONS** ⏱️ PREP TIME | 10 MIN 🔲 COOK TIME | 1 MIN

1 | Combine all ingredients in a large bowl and mix well.
2 | Place the mixture into a loaf in a parchment-lined air fryer basket.
3 | Preheat the air fryer to 350°F (175°C). Cook for 30-35 minutes until internal temperature reaches 160°F (71°C).
4 | Let the meatloaf rest for 10 minutes before slicing.
5 | Slice and serve.

PHILLY **CHEESESTEAK SANDWICHES**

● **INGREDIENTS** 🍽️ YIELDS | 4 SERVES

1 lb thinly sliced ribeye steak
1 small onion, sliced
1 green bell pepper, sliced
1 cup sliced mushrooms
4 slices provolone cheese

4 hoagie rolls
2 tablespoons olive oil
1 teaspoon salt
1/2 teaspoon black pepper

● **DIRECTIONS** ⏱️ PREP TIME | 10 MIN 🔲 COOK TIME | 1 MIN

1 | Combine steak, onion, bell pepper, mushrooms, olive oil, salt, and pepper in a large bowl and mix well.
2 | Preheat the air fryer to 375°F (190°C). Cook the steak and vegetable mixture in the air fryer for 10-12 minutes, stirring halfway through.
3 | Open hoagie rolls and place a slice of provolone cheese in each.
4 | Fill rolls with the cooked steak and vegetable mixture.
5 | Serve hot with crispy fries or a fresh salad.

KOREAN BBQ **SHORT RIBS**

● **INGREDIENTS** 📖 YIELDS | 4 SERVES

2 lbs beef short ribs, cut flanken-style
1/2 cup soy sauce
1/4 cup brown sugar
2 tablespoons sesame oil
4 cloves garlic, minced
1 tablespoon ginger, minced

1 tablespoon rice vinegar
1 tablespoon gochujang (Korean chili paste)
2 green onions, finely chopped
1 tablespoon sesame seeds
Cooking spray

● **DIRECTIONS** ⏱ PREP TIME | 15 MIN 🍳 COOK TIME | 20 MIN

1 | In a large bowl, Combine soy sauce, brown sugar, sesame oil, garlic, ginger, rice vinegar, and gochujang. Add short ribs and coat well—Marinate in the refrigerator for at least 1 hour.
2 | Preheat the air fryer to 375°F (190°C) and lightly spray the basket with cooking spray. Arrange short ribs in a single layer.
3 | Cook for 15-20 minutes, flipping halfway through, until caramelized and tender.
4 | Sprinkle with green onions and sesame seeds before serving.
5 | Serve with steamed rice and kimchi.

JUICY **BEEF TACOS**

● **INGREDIENTS** 📖 YIELDS | 4 SERVES

1 lb ground beef
1 small onion, finely chopped
2 cloves garlic, minced
1 packet taco seasoning mix
1/2 cup water
8 small flour or corn tortillas
1 cup shredded lettuce

1 cup diced tomatoes
1 cup shredded cheddar cheese
1/2 cup sour cream
1/4 cup chopped fresh cilantro
1 lime, cut into wedges
Cooking spray

● **DIRECTIONS** ⏱ PREP TIME | 10 MIN 🍳 COOK TIME | 20 MIN

1 | Preheat the air fryer to 375°F (190°C). In a bowl, mix ground beef, onion, garlic, and taco seasoning. Form into small patties or meatballs.
2 | Lightly spray the air fryer basket with cooking spray. Cook patties or meatballs for 10-12 minutes, flipping halfway.
3 | Lightly spray another layer of the air fryer basket. Warm tortillas for 2-3 minutes.
4 | If necessary, break the beef into smaller pieces. Fill the tortillas with meat, lettuce, tomatoes, cheese, and sour cream.
5 | Sprinkle with cilantro and serve with lime wedges.

SPICY **BEEF EMPANADAS**

● **INGREDIENTS** 🍽 **YIELDS** | 4 SERVES

1 lb ground beef
1 small onion, finely chopped
2 cloves garlic, minced
1 small jalapeño, finely chopped
(optional)
1 packet taco seasoning mix

1/2 cup tomato sauce
1/2 cup shredded cheddar cheese
1 package of empanada dough discs
(store-bought or homemade)
1 egg, beaten (for egg wash)
Cooking spray

● **DIRECTIONS** ⏱ PREP TIME | 20 MIN 📟 COOK TIME | 20 MIN

1 | Cook ground beef, onion, garlic, and jalapeño (if using) in a skillet over medium heat until browned. Drain excess fat. Add taco seasoning and tomato sauce and simmer for 5 minutes. Let cool slightly, then stir in cheese.
2 | Place a spoonful of the beef mixture in the center of each empanada dough disc. Fold over to create a half-moon shape, and seal the edges with a fork. Brush with beaten egg.
3 | Preheat the air fryer to 375°F (190°C). Lightly spray the basket with cooking spray.
4 | Place empanadas in a single layer in the basket, not overlapping. Cook for 12-15 minutes, turning halfway, until golden brown and crispy.
5 | Let cool slightly before serving.

TERIYAKI **BEEF SKEWERS**

● **INGREDIENTS** 🍽 **YIELDS** | 4 SERVES

1 lb beef sirloin, cut into 1-inch cubes
1/2 cup teriyaki sauce
2 tablespoons soy sauce
2 tablespoons honey
2 cloves garlic, minced
1 tablespoon fresh ginger, minced

1 red bell pepper, cut into 1-inch
pieces
1 green bell pepper, cut into 1-inch
pieces
1 small red onion, cut into wedges
Wooden skewers, soaked in water for
30 minutes
Cooking spray

● **DIRECTIONS** ⏱ PREP TIME | 20 MIN 📟 COOK TIME | 15 MIN

1 | Combine teriyaki sauce, soy sauce, honey, garlic, and ginger in a bowl. Add beef cubes, mix well, and marinate in the refrigerator for at least 30 minutes.
2 | Preheat the air fryer to 375°F (190°C).
3 | Thread marinated beef, red bell pepper, green bell pepper, and red onion onto soaked skewers, alternating meat and vegetables.
4 | Lightly spray the air fryer basket with cooking spray. Place skewers in a single layer in the basket, not overlapping.
5 | Cook at 375°F (190°C) for 12-15 minutes, turning halfway, until beef is cooked to desired doneness and vegetables are tender. Let cool slightly before serving.

CLASSIC **CHEESEBURGERS**

● INGREDIENTS 🍽 YIELDS | 4 SERVES

1 lb ground beef (80% lean, 20% fat)
1 teaspoon salt
1/2 teaspoon black pepper
4 slices cheddar cheese
4 hamburger buns
Lettuce leaves

Tomato slices
Pickle slices
Ketchup
Mustard
Cooking spray

● DIRECTIONS ⏱ PREP TIME | 10 MIN 🍳 COOK TIME | 12 MIN

1 | Mix ground beef with salt and pepper. Divide into four patties, about 3/4 inch thick, and make a slight indentation in each center.
2 | Preheat the air fryer to 375°F (190°C).
3 | Lightly spray the air fryer basket with cooking spray. Place patties in a single layer, not overlapping.
4 | Cook at 375°F (190°C) for 8-10 minutes, flipping halfway. In the last minute, place cheddar cheese on each patty to melt.
5 | Lightly toast buns in the air fryer for 1-2 minutes. Assemble burgers with patties, lettuce, tomato, pickles, ketchup, and mustard. Serve immediately.

CRISPY **PORK CHOPS**

● INGREDIENTS 🍽 YIELDS | 4 SERVES

4 bone-in pork chops (about 1 inch thick)
1 teaspoon salt
1/2 teaspoon black pepper
1 cup all-purpose flour
2 eggs, beaten

1 cup panko breadcrumbs
1/2 cup grated Parmesan cheese
1 teaspoon garlic powder
1 teaspoon onion powder
1 teaspoon paprika
Cooking spray

● DIRECTIONS ⏱ PREP TIME | 10 MIN 🍳 COOK TIME | 20 MIN

1 | Preheat the air fryer to 400°F (200°C).
2 | Season pork chops with salt and pepper. Dredge in flour, dip in beaten eggs, and coat with panko, Parmesan, garlic powder, onion powder, and paprika.
3 | Lightly spray the air fryer basket with cooking spray. Place pork chops in a single layer, not overlapping.
4 | Cook at 400°F (200°C) for 15-20 minutes, flipping halfway, until golden brown and internal temperature reaches 145°F (63°C).
5 | Let rest for a few minutes before serving.

SWEET & TANGY BBQ RIBS

● INGREDIENTS  YIELDS | 4 SERVES

2 lbs pork ribs, cut into individual ribs
1 teaspoon salt
1 teaspoon black pepper
2 bay leaves
1 teaspoon black peppercorns
2 cloves garlic, smashed
1 small onion, quartered

For the BBQ Sauce:
1 cup BBQ sauce
1/4 cup honey
2 tablespoons apple cider vinegar
1 tablespoon Worcestershire sauce
1 teaspoon smoked paprika

● DIRECTIONS  PREP TIME | 15 MIN   COOK TIME | 1 HOUR 20 MIN (INCLUDING BOILING TIME)

1 | Place ribs in a pot, cover with water, add salt, bay leaves, peppercorns, garlic, and onion. Boil, then simmer for 45 minutes to 1 hour until tender.
2 | While the ribs simmer, mix BBQ sauce, honey, apple cider vinegar, Worcestershire sauce, and smoked paprika. Set aside.
3 | Preheat the air fryer to 375°F (190°C).
4 | Pat ribs dry and brush generously with BBQ sauce.
5 | Lightly spray the air fryer basket with cooking spray. Place ribs in a single layer and cook for 15-20 minutes, turning halfway and brushing with more BBQ sauce until caramelized. Let rest before serving.

PULLED PORK SLIDERS

● INGREDIENTS  YIELDS | 4 SERVES

2 lbs pork shoulder or pork butt
1 teaspoon salt
1 teaspoon black pepper
1 teaspoon smoked paprika
1 teaspoon garlic powder
1 teaspoon onion powder
1/2 teaspoon cayenne pepper
(optional)

1 cup BBQ sauce
12 slider buns
Coleslaw (optional for serving)
Pickles (optional, for serving)
Cooking spray

● DIRECTIONS  PREP TIME | 15 MIN  COOK TIME | 1 HOUR 30 MIN

1 | Preheat the air fryer to 300°F (150°C). Mix salt, black pepper, smoked paprika, garlic powder, onion powder, and cayenne pepper. Rub the spice mixture on the pork.
2 | Lightly spray the air fryer basket with cooking spray. Place seasoned pork in the basket.
3 | Cook at 300°F (150°C) for 1 hour and 30 minutes or until tender and easily shredded. Check periodically and cover with foil if necessary.
4 | Let the pork rest for 10 minutes, then shred it with two forks. Mix the shredded pork with BBQ sauce.
5 | Lightly toast slider buns in the air fryer for 1-2 minutes. Assemble sliders with pulled pork, coleslaw, and pickles if desired. Serve immediately.

GARLIC **PARMESAN TENDERLOIN**

● INGREDIENTS 🥞 YIELDS | 4 SERVES

1 pork tenderloin (about 1.5 lbs)
3 tablespoons olive oil
4 cloves garlic, minced
1 tablespoon fresh rosemary, chopped
1 tablespoon fresh thyme, chopped

1 teaspoon salt
1 teaspoon black pepper
1/2 cup grated Parmesan cheese (for topping)
Cooking spray

● DIRECTIONS ⏱ PREP TIME | 15 MIN 🍳 COOK TIME | 30 MIN

1 | Mix olive oil, garlic, rosemary, thyme, salt, and black pepper. Rub the mixture over the pork tenderloin. Cover and refrigerate for 30 minutes.
2 | Preheat the air fryer to 375°F (190°C).
3 | Lightly spray the air fryer basket with cooking spray. Place the tenderloin in the basket.
4 | Cook at 375°F (190°C) for 20-25 minutes, turning halfway, until the internal temperature reaches 140°F (60°C).
5 | Sprinkle Parmesan cheese over the tenderloin and cook for another 5 minutes, until the internal temperature reaches 145°F (63°C). Let rest for 10 minutes before slicing.

GOLDEN **PORK SCHNITZEL**

● INGREDIENTS 🥞 YIELDS | 4 SERVES

4 boneless pork chops (about 1/2 inch thick)
1 teaspoon salt
1/2 teaspoon black pepper
1 cup all-purpose flour
2 eggs, beaten
1 cup panko breadcrumbs

1/2 cup grated Parmesan cheese
1 teaspoon garlic powder
1 teaspoon paprika
Cooking spray
Lemon wedges (for serving)

● DIRECTIONS ⏱ PREP TIME | 15 MIN 🍳 COOK TIME | 15 MIN

1 | Pound pork chops to 1/4 inch thickness between plastic wrap. Season with salt and pepper.
2 | In separate bowls, combine flour, beaten eggs, panko, Parmesan, garlic powder, and paprika. Dredge chops in flour, dip in eggs, and coat with breadcrumb mixture.
3 | Preheat the air fryer to 375°F (190°C).
4 | Lightly spray the air fryer basket with cooking spray. Place chops in a single layer. Cook at 375°F (190°C) for 12-15 minutes, flipping halfway, until golden brown and internal temperature reaches 145°F (63°C).
5 | Let rest before serving. Serve with lemon wedges.

MAPLE **GLAZED PORK BELLY**

● **INGREDIENTS** 🍽 **YIELDS | 4 SERVES**

2 lbs pork belly, skin removed
1 teaspoon salt
1/2 teaspoon black pepper
1/4 cup maple syrup
2 tablespoons soy sauce

2 tablespoons Dijon mustard
2 cloves garlic, minced
1 tablespoon apple cider vinegar
1 teaspoon smoked paprika
Cooking spray

● **DIRECTIONS** ⏱ PREP TIME | 15 MIN 📟 COOK TIME | 1 HOUR

1 | Preheat the air fryer to 300°F (150°C). Season pork belly with salt and pepper.
2 | Lightly spray the air fryer basket with cooking spray. Place pork belly in the basket, skin-side down.
3 | Cook at 300°F (150°C) for 45 minutes.
4 | Mix maple syrup, soy sauce, Dijon mustard, garlic, apple cider vinegar, and smoked paprika for the glaze.
5 | Increase temperature to 375°F (190°C). Brush pork belly with glaze and cook for 15 minutes, turning and basting every 5 minutes until caramelized. Let rest for 10 minutes before slicing.

ITALIAN **SAUSAGE & PEPPERS**

● **INGREDIENTS** 🍽 **YIELDS | 4 SERVES**

4 Italian sausages
1 red bell pepper, sliced into strips
1 green bell pepper, sliced into strips
1 yellow bell pepper, sliced into strips
1 large onion, sliced into strips
2 tablespoons olive oil

1 teaspoon Italian seasoning
1 teaspoon garlic powder
1 teaspoon salt
1/2 teaspoon black pepper
Cooking spray

● **DIRECTIONS** ⏱ PREP TIME | 10 MIN 📟 COOK TIME | 20 MIN

1 | In a bowl, toss bell peppers, onion, olive oil, Italian seasoning, garlic powder, salt, and black pepper.
2 | Preheat the air fryer to 375°F (190°C). Lightly spray the basket with cooking spray. Place sausages in a single layer.
3 | Cook sausages for 10 minutes, turning halfway.
4 | Add bell peppers and onions to the basket and stir with sausages. Cook for another 10 minutes, shaking occasionally, until sausages are golden and vegetables are tender.
5 | Let cool slightly before serving.

PORK & APPLE SKEWERS

 INGREDIENTS  YIELDS | 4 SERVES

1 lb pork tenderloin, cut into 1-inch cubes
2 large apples, cored and cut into 1-inch cubes
2 tablespoons olive oil
2 tablespoons apple cider vinegar
Wooden skewers, soaked in water for 30 minutes

2 tablespoons honey
2 cloves garlic, minced
1 teaspoon fresh rosemary, chopped
1 teaspoon fresh thyme, chopped
1 teaspoon salt
1/2 teaspoon black pepper
Cooking spray

 DIRECTIONS ⏱ PREP TIME | 15 MIN 📟 COOK TIME | 15 MIN

1 | In a bowl, mix olive oil, apple cider vinegar, honey, garlic, rosemary, thyme, salt, and pepper. Add pork cubes, toss to coat, and refrigerate for 30 minutes.
2 | Preheat the air fryer to 375°F (190°C).
3 | Thread pork and apple cubes onto soaked skewers, alternating.
4 | Lightly spray the air fryer basket with cooking spray. Place skewers in a single layer.
5 | Cook at 375°F (190°C) for 12-15 minutes, turning halfway, until pork is cooked and apples are tender. Let rest before serving.

JUICY PORK MEATBALLS

 INGREDIENTS  YIELDS | 4 SERVES

1 lb ground pork
1/2 cup breadcrumbs
1/4 cup grated Parmesan cheese
1/4 cup milk
1 egg, beaten
2 cloves garlic, minced

1 small onion, finely chopped
2 tablespoons fresh parsley, chopped
1 teaspoon salt
1/2 teaspoon black pepper
1/2 teaspoon dried oregano
Cooking spray

 DIRECTIONS ⏱ PREP TIME | 15 MIN 📟 COOK TIME | 15 MIN

1 | Preheat the air fryer to 375°F (190°C).
2 | In a bowl, mix ground pork, breadcrumbs, Parmesan, milk, egg, garlic, onion, parsley, salt, pepper, and oregano until well combined. Shape into 1-inch meatballs.
3 | Lightly spray the air fryer basket with cooking spray. Place meatballs in a single layer.
4 | Cook at 375°F (190°C) for 12-15 minutes, shaking the basket halfway through until golden brown and cooked.
5 | Let rest for a few minutes before serving.

PORK TACOS WITH **PINEAPPLE SALSA**

● **INGREDIENTS** 🍽 **YIELDS** | 4 SERVES

1 lb pork tenderloin, cut into thin strips
2 tablespoons olive oil
1 teaspoon ground cumin
1 teaspoon chili powder
1 teaspoon garlic powder
1/2 teaspoon salt
1/2 teaspoon black pepper
8 small flour or corn tortillas

For the Pineapple Salsa:
1 cup fresh pineapple, diced
1/2 red onion, finely chopped
1/2 red bell pepper, diced
1 jalapeño, seeded and finely chopped
1/4 cup fresh cilantro, chopped
1 tablespoon lime juice
Salt to taste

● **DIRECTIONS** ⏱ PREP TIME | 20 MIN 📟 COOK TIME | 15 MIN

1 | Preheat the air fryer to 375°F (190°C).
2 | Toss pork strips with olive oil, cumin, chili powder, garlic powder, salt, and pepper.
3 | Lightly spray the air fryer basket with cooking spray. Cook pork strips in a single layer at 375°F (190°C) for 10-12 minutes, shaking halfway through.
4 | Prepare pineapple salsa by mixing diced pineapple, red onion, bell pepper, jalapeño, cilantro, lime juice, and salt.
5 | Warm tortillas in the air fryer for 1-2 minutes. Assemble tacos with pork and pineapple salsa. Serve immediately.

ROSEMARY **RACK OF LAMB**

● **INGREDIENTS** 🍽 YIELDS | 4 SERVES

1 rack of lamb (about 2 lbs), frenched
2 tablespoons olive oil
3 cloves garlic, minced
2 tablespoons fresh rosemary, chopped

1 tablespoon fresh thyme, chopped
1 teaspoon salt
1/2 teaspoon black pepper
1 teaspoon Dijon mustard
Cooking spray

● **DIRECTIONS** ⏱ PREP TIME | 1 MIN 📟 COOK TIME | 1 MIN

1 | In a bowl, mix olive oil, garlic, rosemary, thyme, salt, pepper, and Dijon mustard. Rub the mixture onto the lamb rack and refrigerate for at least 1 hour.
2 | Preheat the air fryer to 375°F (190°C).
3 | Lightly spray the air fryer basket with cooking spray. Place the lamb rack in the basket, meat side up.
4 | Cook at 375°F (190°C) for 25-30 minutes, turning halfway, until the internal temperature reaches 145°F (63°C) for medium-rare.
5 | Let rest for 10 minutes before slicing into chops. Serve.

MINT & GARLIC **LAMB KEBABS**

● **INGREDIENTS** 🍽 YIELDS | 4 SERVES

1 lb ground lamb
1 small onion, finely chopped
3 cloves garlic, minced
1/4 cup fresh mint, chopped
1/4 cup fresh parsley, chopped
1 tablespoon olive oil
1 teaspoon ground cumin

1 teaspoon ground coriander
1 teaspoon salt
1/2 teaspoon black pepper
Wooden skewers, soaked in water for
30 minutes
Cooking spray

● **DIRECTIONS** ⏱ PREP TIME | 20 MIN 🍳 COOK TIME | 15 MIN

1 | In a bowl, mix ground lamb, onion, garlic, mint, parsley, olive oil, cumin, coriander, salt, and pepper. Refrigerate for 30 minutes.
2 | Preheat the air fryer to 375°F (190°C).
3 | Shape the lamb mixture into oval patties around soaked skewers.
4 | Lightly spray the air fryer basket with cooking spray. Place kebabs in a single layer.
5 | Cook at 375°F (190°C) for 12-15 minutes, turning halfway, until browned and cooked through. Let rest before serving.

MEAT **LOVER'S EGG ROLLS**

● **INGREDIENTS** 🍽 YIELDS | 4 SERVES | 12 EGG ROLLS

1/2 lb ground beef
1/2 lb ground pork
1 cup cooked and crumbled bacon
1 cup shredded mozzarella or cheddar
cheese
1 small onion, finely chopped

2 cloves garlic, minced
1 tablespoon soy sauce
1 teaspoon ground black pepper
1 package egg roll wrappers
1 egg, beaten (for egg wash)
Cooking spray

● **DIRECTIONS** ⏱ PREP TIME | 20 MIN 🍳 COOK TIME | 15 MIN

1 | Cook ground beef and pork in a skillet over medium heat until browned. Drain excess fat.
2 | Add onion and garlic to the skillet. Cook for 5 minutes until softened. Stir in bacon, cheese, soy sauce, and black pepper. Cook for 2-3 minutes until cheese melts. Let cool slightly.
3 | Lay an egg roll wrapper on a flat surface—spoon 2 tablespoons of the meat mixture onto the wrapper. Fold the bottom corner over the filling, fold in the sides, and roll up tightly. Brush the top corner with the beaten egg to seal. Repeat with the remaining wrappers.
4 | Preheat the air fryer to 375°F (190°C).
5 | Lightly spray the air fryer basket with cooking spray. Place the egg rolls in a single layer, not overlapping. Lightly spray the tops with cooking spray. Cook for 12-15 minutes, turning halfway, until golden brown and crispy. Let cool slightly before serving.

STUFFED **BELL PEPPERS**

● INGREDIENTS  YIELDS | 4 SERVES

4 large bell peppers (any color)
1/2 lb ground beef
1/2 lb ground pork
1 small onion, finely chopped
2 cloves garlic, minced
1 cup cooked rice
1 can (14.5 oz) diced tomatoes, drained
1 cup shredded cheddar cheese or mozzarella cheese

1 teaspoon ground cumin
1 teaspoon dried oregano
1/2 teaspoon smoked paprika
1 teaspoon salt
1/2 teaspoon black pepper
2 tablespoons olive oil
1/4 cup fresh parsley, chopped (for garnish)
Cooking spray

● DIRECTIONS ⏱ PREP TIME | 1 MIN 🔲 COOK TIME | 1 MIN

1 | Cut tops off bell peppers and remove seeds and membranes. Brush the insides with olive oil.
2 | Cook ground beef and pork in a skillet until browned. Drain the fat, then add onion and garlic. Cook for 5 minutes.
3 | Stir in cooked rice, diced tomatoes, cumin, oregano, smoked paprika, salt, and black pepper. Cook for 2-3 minutes. Remove from heat and stir in half of the cheese.
4 | Preheat the air fryer to 375°F (190°C).
5 | Stuff bell peppers with the meat mixture. Lightly spray the air fryer basket with cooking spray. Place peppers in a single layer.
6 | Cook at 375°F (190°C) for 20-25 minutes. Add the remaining cheese and cook for 5 minutes until melted and bubbly. Let cool before serving. Garnish with parsley.

MEAT **LOVER'S PIZZA**

● INGREDIENTS YIELDS | 4 SERVES

1 pre-made pizza dough (or homemade)
1/2 cup pizza sauce
1 1/2 cups shredded mozzarella cheese
1/2 cup cooked sausage, crumbled
1/2 cup cooked ground beef

1/2 cup pepperoni slices
1/2 cup cooked bacon, crumbled
1/4 cup ham, diced
1 teaspoon dried oregano
1 teaspoon dried basil
Cooking spray

● DIRECTIONS ⏱ PREP TIME | 15 MIN 🔲 COOK TIME | 15 MIN

1 | Preheat the air fryer to 375°F (190°C).
2 | Roll out the pizza dough to fit the air fryer basket.
3 | Lightly spray the basket with cooking spray and place the dough inside.
4 | Spread pizza sauce on the dough, then sprinkle half of the mozzarella cheese.
5 | Add sausage, ground beef, pepperoni, bacon, and ham. Top with remaining cheese, oregano, and basil.
6 | Air fry at 375°F (190°C) for 12-15 minutes until the crust is golden and the cheese is bubbly.
7 | Let cool before slicing and serving.

MEAT STUFFED MUSHROOMS

 INGREDIENTS  YIELDS | 4 SERVES

2 large button mushrooms or cremini mushrooms
1/2 lb ground beef
1/2 lb ground pork
1 small onion, finely chopped
2 cloves garlic, minced
1/4 cup breadcrumbs

1/4 cup grated Parmesan cheese
1/4 cup cream cheese, softened
2 tablespoons fresh parsley, chopped
1 teaspoon dried oregano
1 teaspoon salt
1/2 teaspoon black pepper
Cooking spray

● DIRECTIONS ⏱ PREP TIME | 15 MIN 🍳 COOK TIME | 20 MIN

1 | Clean mushrooms and remove stems. Finely chop stems and set aside.
2 | Cook ground beef and pork in a skillet over medium heat until browned. Drain excess fat.
3 | Add onion, garlic, and mushroom stems to the skillet. Cook for 5 minutes until softened. Stir in breadcrumbs, Parmesan, cream cheese, parsley, oregano, salt, and pepper. Cook for 2-3 minutes until combined. Let cool slightly.
4 | Preheat the air fryer to 375°F (190°C).
5 | Stuff each mushroom cap with the meat mixture. Lightly spray the air fryer basket with cooking spray. Place stuffed mushrooms in a single layer.
6 | Cook at 375°F (190°C) for 15-20 minutes until mushrooms are tender and the filling is golden brown. Let cool before serving. Garnish with parsley if desired.

HOMESTYLE BEEF MEATLOAF

● INGREDIENTS 🍽 YIELDS | 4 SERVES

1 pound ground beef
1 small onion, finely chopped
1/2 cup breadcrumbs
1/4 cup milk
1 large egg
2 cloves garlic, minced
2 tablespoons ketchup
1 tablespoon Worcestershire sauce

1 teaspoon dried thyme
1 teaspoon salt
1/2 teaspoon black pepper
For the Glaze:
1/4 cup ketchup
2 tablespoons brown sugar
1 tablespoon Dijon mustard

● DIRECTIONS ⏱ PREP TIME | 15 MIN 🍳 COOK TIME | 25 MIN

1 | Combine ground beef, onion, breadcrumbs, milk, egg, garlic, ketchup, Worcestershire sauce, thyme, salt, and pepper in a bowl. Mix until just combined.
2 | Shape the mixture into a loaf that fits your air fryer basket.
3 | Preheat the air fryer to 350°F (175°C) for about 5 minutes.
4 | Lightly spray the air fryer basket with cooking spray. Place the meatloaf in the basket and cook for 20 minutes.
5 | Mix ketchup, brown sugar, and Dijon mustard to prepare the glaze.
6 | After 20 minutes, spread the glaze over the meatloaf. Continue cooking for 5-10 minutes until the internal temperature reaches 160°F (71°C).
7 | Let the meatloaf rest for 5 minutes before slicing and serving.

CLASSIC **CHILI CON CARNE**

● **INGREDIENTS** YIELDS | 4 SERVES

1 lb ground beef
1/2 lb ground pork
1 large onion, chopped
3 cloves garlic, minced
1 red bell pepper, chopped
1 green bell pepper, chopped
1 jalapeño, seeded and finely chopped (optional)
2 tablespoons olive oil
2 tablespoons chili powder
1 tablespoon ground cumin
1 tablespoon paprika
1 teaspoon dried oregano
1 teaspoon salt
1/2 teaspoon black pepper

1/4 teaspoon cayenne pepper (optional)
1 can (14.5 oz) diced tomatoes
1 can (15 oz) kidney beans, drained and rinsed
1 can (15 oz) black beans, drained and rinsed
1 can (6 oz) tomato paste
1 cup beef broth
1 tablespoon Worcestershire sauce
Fresh cilantro, chopped (for garnish)
Sour cream (for serving)
Shredded cheddar cheese (for serving)
Cooking spray

● **DIRECTIONS** PREP TIME | 1 MIN 🔲COOK TIME | 1 MIN

1 | Preheat the air fryer to 375°F (190°C). Lightly spray the air fryer basket with cooking spray.
2 | Cook ground beef and pork in the basket for 10-12 minutes, stirring halfway until browned. Drain excess fat and set aside.
3 | Cook onion, garlic, bell peppers, and jalapeño (if using) in the air fryer at 375°F (190°C) for 5-7 minutes until softened.
4 | Return meat to the basket, add spices (chili powder, cumin, paprika, oregano, salt, black pepper, cayenne), and cook for 2-3 minutes until fragrant.
5 | Add diced tomatoes, kidney beans, black beans, tomato paste, beef broth, and Worcestershire sauce. Stir to combine. Reduce temperature to 325°F (160°C) and cook for 15-20 minutes, stirring occasionally. Cover if possible.
6 | Adjust seasoning if needed. Serve hot, garnished with cilantro, sour cream, and shredded cheddar cheese.

AIR FRYER FISH FEAST

CRISPY SALMON FILLETS

● INGREDIENTS  YIELDS | 4 SERVES

4 salmon fillets (about 6 oz each)
1/4 cup grated Parmesan cheese
1/4 cup panko breadcrumbs
2 tablespoons pesto sauce (for pesto variation)
2 tablespoons mayonnaise (for pesto variation)

2 tablespoons olive oil
1 tablespoon lemon juice
Salt and pepper to taste
Cooking spray

● DIRECTIONS ⏱ PREP TIME | 15 MIN ⬛ COOK TIME | 15 MIN

1 | Preheat the air fryer to 400°F (200°C) for about 5 minutes.
2 | Mix the grated Parmesan cheese and panko breadcrumbs in a small bowl.
3 | For the Parmesan Crusted Salmon:
Pat the salmon fillets dry with paper towels. Lightly season each fillet with salt and pepper.
Press the Parmesan-panko mixture onto the top of each fillet to create a crust.
4 | For the Pesto Crusted Salmon:
In another small bowl, combine the pesto sauce and mayonnaise.
Pat the salmon fillets dry with paper towels. Lightly season each fillet with salt and pepper.
Brush each salmon fillet with the pesto-mayonnaise mixture, ensuring an even coat. Press the Parmesan-panko mixture onto the top of each fillet to create a crust.
5 | Lightly spray the air fryer basket with cooking spray. Arrange the salmon fillets in a single layer, crust side up, in the basket.
6 | Drizzle the fillets with olive oil and lemon juice to enhance flavor and crispiness.
7 | Cook at 400°F (200°C) for 10-12 minutes until the salmon cooks through and the crust turns golden brown and crispy. The internal temperature should reach 145°F (63°C).
8 | Remove the salmon fillets from the air fryer and let them rest for a few minutes before serving.

HONEY-GARLIC **GLAZED TILAPIA**

● **INGREDIENTS** 🍽 **YIELDS | 4 SERVES**

4 tilapia fillets
1/4 cup honey
3 cloves garlic, minced
 Green onions and sesame seeds for garnish

2 tablespoons soy sauce
1 tablespoon olive oil
1 teaspoon fresh ginger, grated
Salt and pepper to taste

● **DIRECTIONS** ⏱ **PREP TIME | 10 MIN** 🍳 **COOK TIME | 10 MIN**

1 | Whisk together the honey, minced garlic, soy sauce, olive oil, grated ginger, salt, and pepper in a small bowl.
2 | Place the tilapia fillets in a shallow dish and pour the honey-garlic glaze over them. Ensure the fillets are well coated. Let them marinate for 10-15 minutes for better flavor.
3 | Preheat the air fryer to 375°F (190°C).
4 | Place the tilapia fillets in the air fryer basket in a single layer. Cook for 8-10 minutes until the fish cooks through and flakes easily with a fork.
5 | Sprinkle with chopped green onions and sesame seeds before serving.
6 | Serve hot with your favorite sides.

CAJUN-SPICED **CATFISH NUGGETS**

● **INGREDIENTS** 🍽 **YIELDS | 4 SERVES**

1-pound catfish fillets, cut into nuggets
1/2 cup cornmeal
1/4 cup flour
2 tablespoons Cajun seasoning

1 teaspoon garlic powder
Salt and pepper to taste
Cooking spray

● **DIRECTIONS** ⏱ **PREP TIME | 10 MIN** 🍳 **COOK TIME | 12 MIN**

1 | Season the catfish nuggets with salt and pepper.
2 | Combine the cornmeal, flour, Cajun seasoning, and garlic powder in a bowl.
3 | Coat the seasoned catfish nuggets with the cornmeal mixture, ensuring they are well-covered.
4 | Preheat the air fryer to 375°F (190°C).
5 | Spray the air fryer basket with cooking spray. Place the nuggets in the basket in a single layer. Cook for 10-12 minutes, shaking the basket halfway through, until the nuggets are golden and crispy.
6 | Serve hot with your favorite dipping sauce.

LEMON DILL COD

● INGREDIENTS 🍲 YIELDS | 4 SERVES

4 cod fillets
2 tablespoons olive oil, divided
1 lemon, juiced and zested
2 teaspoons dried dill
1 teaspoon garlic powder

Salt and pepper to taste
1 cup cherry tomatoes, halved
1 cup zucchini, sliced
1 cup bell peppers, sliced

● DIRECTIONS ⏱ PREP TIME | 15 MIN 🔲 COOK TIME | 12 MIN

1 | Season the cod fillets with salt and pepper. Mix 1 tablespoon olive oil, lemon juice, lemon zest, dried dill, and garlic powder in a small bowl. Coat the cod fillets with this mixture.
2 | In a separate bowl, toss the cherry tomatoes, zucchini, and bell peppers with the remaining 1 tablespoon olive oil, salt, and pepper.
3 | Preheat the air fryer to 375°F (190°C).
4 | Place the cod fillets and vegetables in the air fryer basket in a single layer. Cook for 10-12 minutes until the fish flakes easily with a fork and the vegetables are tender.
5 | Serve hot with the roasted vegetables.

SPICY SRIRACHA SHRIMP SKEWERS

● INGREDIENTS 🍲 YIELDS | 4 SERVES

1 pound large shrimp, peeled and deveined
2 tablespoons sriracha sauce
1 tablespoon honey

1 tablespoon soy sauce
1 teaspoon garlic powder
1 teaspoon lime juice
Salt and pepper to taste

● DIRECTIONS ⏱ PREP TIME | 15 MIN 🔲 COOK TIME | 8 MIN

1 | Season the shrimp with salt and pepper. Mix the Sriracha sauce, honey, soy sauce, garlic powder, and lime juice in a small bowl. Coat the shrimp with this mixture and let them marinate for 10-15 minutes.
2 | Preheat the air fryer to 375°F (190°C).
3 | Thread the shrimp onto skewers.
4 | Place the shrimp skewers in the air fryer basket in a single layer. Cook for 6-8 minutes, turning halfway through, until the shrimp become slightly charred and cook through.
5 | Serve hot with lime wedges.

HERB-CRUSTED **SEA BASS**

● **INGREDIENTS** 🍽 YIELDS | 4 SERVES

4 sea bass fillets
1/4 cup breadcrumbs
2 tablespoons grated Parmesan
cheese
1 tablespoon fresh parsley, chopped
1 tablespoon fresh oregano, chopped

1 tablespoon fresh basil, chopped
2 cloves garlic, minced
1 tablespoon olive oil
Salt and pepper to taste
Lemon wedges for serving

● **DIRECTIONS** ⏱ PREP TIME | 15 MIN 🍳 COOK TIME | 12 MIN

1 | Season the sea bass fillets with salt and pepper. Mix the breadcrumbs, grated Parmesan cheese, parsley, oregano, basil, garlic, and olive oil in a small bowl to form the herb crust mixture.
2 | Coat the sea bass fillets with the herb crust mixture, pressing gently to ensure it sticks.
3 | Preheat the air fryer to 375°F (190°C).
4 | Place the sea bass fillets in the air fryer basket in a single layer. Cook for 10-12 minutes or until the fish is golden and cooked through.
5 | Serve hot with lemon wedges.

CLASSIC **FISH AND CHIPS**

● **INGREDIENTS** 🍽 YIELDS | 4 SERVES

4 cod fillets
1 cup all-purpose flour, divided
1 teaspoon baking powder
1 cup cold sparkling water
1 teaspoon salt, divided
1/2 teaspoon black pepper

1/2 teaspoon paprika
1/2 teaspoon garlic powder
2 large potatoes, cut into fries
Cooking spray
Malt vinegar and tartar sauce for
serving

● **DIRECTIONS** ⏱ PREP TIME | 20 MIN 🍳 COOK TIME | 20 MIN

1 | Season the cod fillets with 1/2 teaspoon salt, black pepper, paprika, and garlic powder.
2 | In a bowl, mix 3/4 cup flour and baking powder. Add the cold sparkling water gradually, whisking until the batter is smooth.
3 | Coat the seasoned cod fillets in the remaining 1/4 cup flour, shaking off excess, then dip them into the batter, ensuring they are well coated.
4 | Preheat the air fryer to 375°F (190°C).
5 | Spray the air fryer basket with cooking spray. Place the coated cod fillets in the air fryer basket in a single layer. Cook for 10-12 minutes, turning halfway through, until the fish is golden and crispy.
6 | Place the potato fries in the air fryer basket in a single layer in another batch. Spray with cooking spray and season with the remaining 1/2 teaspoon salt. Cook for 15-20 minutes, shaking the basket halfway through, until the fries are golden and crispy.
7 | Serve the fish and chips hot with malt vinegar and tartar sauce.

COCONUT-CRUSTED **TILAPIA TACOS**

● **INGREDIENTS** 🍽 **YIELDS** | 4 SERVES

4 tilapia fillets
1/2 cup shredded coconut
1/2 cup panko breadcrumbs
2 tablespoons flour
2 eggs, beaten
Salt and pepper to taste

8 small taco tortillas
1 cup shredded cabbage
1/2 cup diced mango
1/4 cup chopped cilantro
1/4 cup lime juice
1/4 cup sour cream

● **DIRECTIONS** ⏱ PREP TIME | 15 MIN 🍳 COOK TIME | 12 MIN

1 | Season the tilapia fillets with salt and pepper. Mix the shredded coconut, panko breadcrumbs, and flour in a shallow dish.
2 | Dip each tilapia fillet in the beaten eggs, then coat with the coconut mixture, pressing gently to adhere.
3 | Preheat the air fryer to 375°F (190°C).
4 | Place the coated tilapia fillets in the air fryer basket in a single layer. Cook for 10-12 minutes or until the fish is golden and cooked through.
5 | While the fish is cooking, prepare the taco toppings by mixing the shredded cabbage, diced mango, chopped cilantro, and lime juice.
6 | Once you cook the fish, cut the fillets into smaller pieces suitable for tacos.
7 | Assemble the tacos by placing the fish pieces on the tortillas, then topping with the cabbage mixture and a dollop of sour cream.
8 | Serve immediately.

GARLIC **BUTTER SCALLOPS**

● **INGREDIENTS** 🍽 YIELDS | 4 SERVES

1 pound sea scallops
2 tablespoons butter, melted
3 cloves garlic, minced
1 tablespoon olive oil

1 teaspoon lemon juice
Salt and pepper to taste
Fresh parsley, chopped, for garnish

● **DIRECTIONS** ⏱ PREP TIME | 10 MIN 🍳 COOK TIME | 10 MIN

1 | Season the scallops with salt and pepper. Mix the melted butter, minced garlic, olive oil, and lemon juice in a small bowl.
2 | Coat the scallops with the garlic butter mixture.
3 | Preheat the air fryer to 375°F (190°C).
4 | Place the scallops in the air fryer basket in a single layer. Cook for 8-10 minutes, shaking the basket halfway through, until the scallops are golden and cooked.
5 | Sprinkle with chopped parsley before serving.
6 | Serve hot.

CAJUN **BLACKENED RED SNAPPER**

● **INGREDIENTS** 🥞 YIELDS | 4 SERVES

4 red snapper fillets
2 tablespoons olive oil
2 tablespoons Cajun seasoning
1 teaspoon paprika
1 teaspoon garlic powder

1 teaspoon onion powder
1/2 teaspoon dried thyme
1/2 teaspoon dried oregano
Salt and pepper to taste
Lemon wedges for serving

● **DIRECTIONS** ⏱ PREP TIME | 10 MIN 📟 COOK TIME | 12 MIN

1 | In a small bowl, mix the Cajun seasoning, paprika, garlic powder, onion powder, dried thyme, oregano, salt, and pepper.
2 | Rub the red snapper fillets with olive oil, then coat evenly with the seasoning mixture.
3 | Preheat the air fryer to 375°F (190°C).
4 | Place the seasoned red snapper fillets in the air fryer basket in a single layer. Cook for 10-12 minutes until the fish cooks through and flakes easily with a fork.
5 | Serve hot with lemon wedges.

GARLIC **PARMESAN SHRIMP**

● **INGREDIENTS** 🥞 YIELDS | 4 SERVES

1 pound large shrimp, peeled and deveined
3 cloves garlic, minced
1/4 cup grated Parmesan cheese
2 tablespoons olive oil

1 tablespoon fresh parsley, chopped
1 teaspoon lemon juice
Salt and pepper to taste
Lemon wedges for serving

● **DIRECTIONS** ⏱ PREP TIME | 10 MIN 📟 COOK TIME | 10 MIN

1 | Season the shrimp with salt and pepper. Mix the minced garlic, grated Parmesan cheese, olive oil, fresh parsley, and lemon juice in a small bowl.
2 | Coat the shrimp with the garlic Parmesan mixture.
3 | Preheat the air fryer to 375°F (190°C).
4 | Place the shrimp in the air fryer basket in a single layer. Cook for 8-10 minutes, shaking the basket halfway through, until the shrimp are golden and cooked.
5 | Serve hot with lemon wedges.

BAJA FISH TACOS

● INGREDIENTS YIELDS | 4 SERVES

4 tilapia fillets
1/2 cup all-purpose flour
1/2 teaspoon salt
1/2 teaspoon black pepper
1/2 teaspoon paprika
1/2 teaspoon garlic powder
2 eggs, beaten
1/2 cup panko breadcrumbs
8 small taco tortillas

1 cup shredded cabbage
1/2 cup diced tomatoes
1/4 cup diced red onion
1/4 cup chopped cilantro
1 jalapeño, seeded and diced
1 lime, juiced
Salt to taste
Sour cream or crema for serving
Lime wedges for serving

● DIRECTIONS PREP TIME | 20 MIN COOK TIME | 12 MIN

1 | Season the tilapia fillets with salt, black pepper, paprika, and garlic powder. Dredge the fillets in flour, dip them in beaten eggs, and coat them with panko breadcrumbs.
2 | Preheat the air fryer to 375°F (190°C).
3 | Place the breaded tilapia fillets in the air fryer basket in a single layer. Cook for 10-12 minutes, turning halfway through, until the fish is golden and cooked through.
4 | While the fish is cooking, prepare the fresh salsa by combining the diced tomatoes, red onion, cilantro, jalapeño, lime juice, and salt to taste in a bowl.
5 | Once you cook the fish, cut the fillets into smaller pieces suitable for tacos.
6 | Assemble the tacos by placing the fish pieces on the tortillas, then topping them with shredded cabbage, fresh salsa, and a sour cream or crema dollop.
7 | Serve immediately with lime wedges.

LEMON PEPPER TILAPIA

● INGREDIENTS YIELDS | 4 SERVES

4 tilapia fillets
2 tablespoons olive oil
1 lemon, juiced and zested
1 teaspoon lemon pepper seasoning

1 teaspoon garlic powder
Salt to taste
Fresh parsley, chopped, for garnish
Lemon wedges for serving

● DIRECTIONS PREP TIME | 10 MIN COOK TIME | 10 MIN

1 | Season the tilapia fillets with salt, lemon pepper seasoning, and garlic powder. Drizzle with olive oil, lemon juice, and lemon zest.
2 | Preheat the air fryer to 375°F (190°C).
3 | Place the seasoned tilapia fillets in the air fryer basket in a single layer. Cook for 8-10 minutes until the fish cooks through and flakes easily with a fork.
4 | Garnish with chopped fresh parsley before serving.
5 | Serve hot with lemon wedges.

CAJUN-SPICED SHRIMP SKEWERS

● INGREDIENTS 🥞 YIELDS | 4 SERVES

1 pound large shrimp, peeled and
deveined
2 tablespoons olive oil
1 tablespoon Cajun seasoning
1 teaspoon garlic powder
1 teaspoon smoked paprika

Salt and pepper to taste
Lemon wedges for serving
Fresh parsley, chopped, for garnish
Skewers (if using wooden skewers,
soak in water for 30 minutes)

● DIRECTIONS ⏱ PREP TIME | 15 MIN 🔲 COOK TIME | 10 MIN

1 | Toss the shrimp with olive oil, Cajun seasoning, garlic powder, smoked paprika, salt, and pepper until well coated in a large bowl.
2 | Thread the seasoned shrimp onto the skewers.
3 | Preheat the air fryer to 375°F (190°C).
4 | Place the shrimp skewers in the air fryer basket in a single layer. Cook for 8-10 minutes, turning halfway through, until the shrimp become slightly charred and cook through.
5 | Garnish with chopped fresh parsley before serving. Serve hot with lemon wedges.

PESTO FISH ROLL

● INGREDIENTS 🥞 YIELDS | 4 SERVES

4 large white fish fillets (such as sole
or flounder)
1/4 cup pesto sauce
1/4 cup sun-dried tomatoes, chopped
1/4 cup breadcrumbs
1/4 cup grated Parmesan cheese

2 cloves garlic, minced
1 tablespoon olive oil
Salt and pepper to taste
Cooking spray
Fresh basil, chopped, for garnish
Lemon wedges for serving

● DIRECTIONS ⏱ PREP TIME | 20 MIN 🔲 COOK TIME | 20 MIN

1 | In a medium bowl, mix the pesto sauce, chopped sun-dried tomatoes, breadcrumbs, grated Parmesan cheese, minced garlic, olive oil, salt, and pepper until well combined.
2 | Lay each fish fillet flat and place a generous spoonful of the pesto and sun-dried tomato mixture on one end. Roll up the fillet tightly and secure it with a toothpick if necessary.
3 | Preheat the air fryer to 375°F (190°C).
4 | While the air fryer is preheating, lightly spray the outside of the rolled fish with cooking spray.
5 | Spray the air fryer basket with cooking spray. Place the stuffed fish roulades in the air fryer basket in a single layer.
6 | Cook for 15-20 minutes until the fish is cooked through and the filling is hot and slightly golden.
7 | Remove the toothpicks if used and garnish with chopped fresh basil before serving. Serve hot with lemon wedges.

LEMON-GARLIC **STUFFED SEA BASS**

● **INGREDIENTS** 🍽 YIELDS | 4 SERVES

4 sea bass fillets
1 cup fresh spinach, chopped
1/4 cup breadcrumbs
1/4 cup grated Parmesan cheese
2 cloves garlic, minced

1 lemon, juiced and zested
2 tablespoons olive oil
Salt and pepper to taste
Fresh parsley, chopped, for garnish
Lemon wedges for serving

● **DIRECTIONS** ⏱ PREP TIME | 20 MIN 🍳 COOK TIME | 20 MIN

1 | Preheat the air fryer to 375°F (190°C).
2 | Mix the chopped spinach, breadcrumbs, grated Parmesan cheese, minced garlic, lemon juice, lemon zest, olive oil, salt, and pepper in a medium bowl.
3 | Carefully cut a pocket in the side of each sea bass fillet. Stuff each fillet with the spinach mixture.
4 | Spray the air fryer basket with cooking spray. Place the stuffed sea bass fillets in the air fryer basket in a single layer.
5 | Cook for 15-20 minutes until the sea bass cooks through and flakes easily with a fork.
6 | Garnish with chopped fresh parsley before serving. Serve hot with lemon wedges.

STUFFED **SOLE FILLETS**

● **INGREDIENTS** 🍽 YIELDS | 4 SERVES

4 sole fillets
1 cup crab meat, cooked and shredded
1/2 cup asparagus, chopped
1/4 cup breadcrumbs
1/4 cup grated Parmesan cheese
2 tablespoons mayonnaise

1 tablespoon fresh lemon juice
2 cloves garlic, minced
1 tablespoon fresh parsley, chopped
Salt and pepper to taste
Cooking spray
Lemon wedges for serving

● **DIRECTIONS** ⏱ PREP TIME | 20 MIN 🍳 COOK TIME | 18 MIN

1 | Preheat the air fryer to 375°F (190°C).
2 | In a medium bowl, mix the crab meat, chopped asparagus, breadcrumbs, grated Parmesan cheese, mayonnaise, lemon juice, minced garlic, chopped parsley, salt, and pepper until well combined.
3 | Lay each sole fillet flat and place a generous spoonful of the crab mixture on one end. Roll up the fillet and secure it with a toothpick if necessary.
4 | Spray the air fryer basket with cooking spray. Place the stuffed sole fillets in the air fryer basket in a single layer.
5 | Cook for 15-18 minutes until the sole cooks through and the stuffing becomes hot and slightly crispy. Remove the toothpicks if used and serve hot with lemon wedges.

SHRIMP **PINEAPPLE ROLLS**

● **INGREDIENTS** YIELDS | 4 SERVES

1 pound large shrimp, peeled and deveined
1/2 cup flour
2 eggs, beaten
1 cup shredded coconut
1/2 cup panko breadcrumbs
Salt and pepper to taste
4 sheets nori (seaweed)
2 cups sushi rice, cooked and seasoned

1 cucumber, julienned
1 avocado, sliced
Cooking spray
Pineapple Dip:
1 cup pineapple, finely chopped
1/4 cup mayonnaise
1 tablespoon lime juice
1 tablespoon honey
Salt to taste

● **DIRECTIONS** PREP TIME | 20 MIN COOK TIME | 12 MIN

1 | Mix the chopped pineapple, mayonnaise, lime juice, honey, and salt in a small bowl. Set aside.
2 | Season the shrimp with salt and pepper. Set up a breading station with three shallow bowls: one with flour, one with beaten eggs, and one with a mixture of shredded coconut and panko breadcrumbs. **3 |** Dredge each shrimp in flour, dip in beaten eggs, and then coat with the coconut-panko mixture, pressing gently to adhere. **4 |** Preheat the air fryer to 375°F (190°C).
5 | Spray the air fryer basket with cooking spray. Place the breaded shrimp in the basket in a single layer. Cook for 10-12 minutes, turning halfway through, until the shrimp are golden and crispy.
6 | Shiny side down lay a sheet of nori on a bamboo sushi mat. Spread a thin layer of sushi rice evenly over the nori, leaving a 1-inch border at the top edge. **7 |** Arrange the cooked coconut shrimp, cucumber, and avocado slices horizontally across the middle of the rice. **8 |** Roll the sushi tightly using the bamboo mat, applying gentle pressure to shape the roll. **9 |** Slice the roll into 8 pieces using a sharp knife. Serve the coconut shrimp rolls with the pineapple dip.

CITRUS **GLAZED SALMON**

● **INGREDIENTS** YIELDS | 4 SERVES

4 salmon fillets
1/4 cup honey
2 tablespoons lime juice
1 tablespoon soy sauce
1 tablespoon olive oil

2 cloves garlic, minced
1 teaspoon lime zest
Salt and pepper to taste
Fresh cilantro, chopped, for garnish
Lime wedges for serving

● **DIRECTIONS** PREP TIME | 10 MIN COOK TIME | 12 MIN

1 | Season the salmon fillets with salt and pepper. Mix the honey, lime juice, soy sauce, olive oil, minced garlic, and zest in a small bowl.
2 | Coat the salmon fillets with the honey lime mixture, ensuring they are well covered.
3 | Preheat the air fryer to 375°F (190°C).
4 | Place the salmon fillets in the air fryer basket in a single layer. Cook 10-12 minutes or until the salmon is cooked and caramelized on the edges.
5 | Garnish with chopped fresh cilantro before serving. Serve hot with lime wedges.

MEDITERRANEAN **FISH ROLLS**

● INGREDIENTS YIELDS | 4 SERVES

4 large white fish fillets (such as sole
or flounder)
1 cup fresh spinach, chopped
1/2 cup feta cheese, crumbled
1/4 cup sun-dried tomatoes, chopped
2 cloves garlic, minced
1 tablespoon olive oil

1 lemon, juiced and zested
1 teaspoon dried oregano
Salt and pepper to taste
Cooking spray
Fresh parsley, chopped, for garnish
Lemon wedges for serving

● DIRECTIONS PREP TIME | 20 MIN COOK TIME | 20 MIN

1 | In a medium bowl, mix the chopped spinach, crumbled feta cheese, chopped sun-dried
tomatoes, minced garlic, olive oil, lemon juice, lemon zest, dried oregano, salt, and pepper until
well combined.
2 | Lay each fish fillet flat and place a generous spoonful of the spinach and feta mixture on one
end. Roll up the fillet tightly and secure it with a toothpick if necessary.
3 | Preheat the air fryer to 375°F (190°C).
4 | While the air fryer is preheating, lightly spray the outside of the rolled fish with cooking spray.
5 | Spray the air fryer basket with cooking spray. Place the stuffed fish roulades in the air fryer
basket in a single layer.
6 | Cook for 15-20 minutes until the fish is cooked through and the filling is hot and slightly golden.
7 | Remove the toothpicks if used and garnish with chopped fresh parsley before serving. Serve
hot with lemon wedges.

QUINOA **STUFFED SALMON**

● INGREDIENTS YIELDS | 4 SERVES

4 salmon fillets
1 cup cooked quinoa
1 cup fresh spinach, chopped
1/4 cup feta cheese, crumbled
2 cloves garlic, minced
1 tablespoon olive oil

1 lemon, juiced and zested
Salt and pepper to taste
Cooking spray
Fresh dill for garnish
Lemon wedges for serving

● DIRECTIONS PREP TIME | 20 MIN COOK TIME | 20 MIN

1 | Preheat the air fryer to 375°F (190°C).
2 | Mix the cooked quinoa, chopped spinach, feta cheese, minced garlic, olive oil, lemon juice,
lemon zest, salt, and pepper in a medium bowl.
3 | Carefully cut a pocket in the side of each salmon fillet. Stuff each fillet with the quinoa and
spinach mixture.
4 | Spray the air fryer basket with cooking spray. Place the stuffed salmon fillets in the air fryer
basket in a single layer.
5 | Cook for 15-20 minutes until the salmon cooks through and flakes easily with a fork.
6 | Garnish with fresh dill before serving. Serve hot with lemon wedges.

CRISPY **SHRIMP ROLLS**

● **INGREDIENTS** 🍽 YIELDS | 4 SERVES

1 pound large shrimp, peeled and
deveined
1 cup tempura batter mix
1 cup cold water
4 sheets nori (seaweed)
2 cups sushi rice, cooked and seasoned

1 avocado, sliced
Soy sauce for serving
Pickled ginger for serving
Wasabi for serving
Cooking spray

● **DIRECTIONS** ⏱ PREP TIME | 30 MIN 🔲 COOK TIME | 10 MIN

1 | Mix the tempura batter with cold water in a small bowl until smooth. Dip the shrimp in the tempura batter, allowing any excess to drip off.
2 | Preheat the air fryer to 375°F (190°C).
3 | Spray the air fryer basket with cooking spray. Place the battered shrimp in the basket in a single layer. Cook for 8-10 minutes or until the shrimp are golden and crispy.
4 | Shiny side down, lay a sheet of nori on a bamboo sushi mat. Spread an even layer of sushi rice over the nori, leaving a 1-inch border at the top edge.
5 | Arrange the cooked tempura shrimp and avocado slices horizontally across the middle of the rice.
6 | Roll the sushi tightly using the bamboo mat, applying gentle pressure to shape the roll.
7 | Slice the roll into 8 pieces using a sharp knife.
8 | Repeat with the remaining nori, rice, tempura shrimp, and avocado.
9 | Serve the crispy tempura shrimp sushi rolls with soy sauce, pickled ginger, and wasabi.

SALMON **CREAM CHEESE ROLLS**

● **INGREDIENTS** 🍽 YIELDS | 4 SERVES

1 pound sushi-grade salmon fillet, cut
into strips
4 sheets nori (seaweed)
2 cups sushi rice, cooked and
seasoned
1/2 cup cream cheese, softened

1 avocado, sliced
1/2 cup panko breadcrumbs
Soy sauce for serving
Pickled ginger for serving
Wasabi for serving
Cooking spray

● **DIRECTIONS** ⏱ PREP TIME | 20 MIN 🔲 COOK TIME | 10 MIN

1 | Preheat the air fryer to 375°F (190°C). **2 |** Lightly spray the salmon strips with cooking spray and coat them in panko breadcrumbs. **3 |** Place the breaded salmon strips in the air fryer basket in a single layer. Cook for 8-10 minutes until the salmon is cooked through and the breadcrumbs are crispy. Let them cool slightly. **4 |** Shiny side down lay a sheet of nori on a bamboo sushi mat. Spread an even layer of sushi rice over the nori, leaving a 1-inch border at the top edge. **5 |** Arrange the cooked salmon strips, cream cheese, and avocado slices horizontally across the middle of the rice. **6 |** Roll the sushi tightly using the bamboo mat, applying gentle pressure to shape the roll. **7 |** Slice the roll into 8 pieces using a sharp knife. **8 |** Repeat with the remaining nori, rice, salmon, cream cheese, and avocado. **9 |** Serve the baked salmon cream cheese rolls with soy sauce, pickled ginger, and wasabi.

SPICY **TUNA CRUNCH ROLLS**

● **INGREDIENTS** 🥞 **YIELDS** | 4 SERVES

1 pound sushi-grade tuna, finely
chopped
2 tablespoons sriracha sauce
1 tablespoon mayonnaise
4 sheets nori (seaweed)
2 cups sushi rice, cooked and
seasoned

1 avocado, sliced
1/2 cup panko breadcrumbs
1 carrot, julienned
Soy sauce for serving
Pickled ginger for serving
Wasabi for serving
Cooking spray

● **DIRECTIONS** ⏱ PREP TIME | 20 MIN 🍳 COOK TIME | 12 MIN

1 | Mix the chopped tuna, sriracha sauce, and mayonnaise in a small bowl until well combined.
2 | Preheat the air fryer to 375°F (190°C).
3 | Shiny side down lay a sheet of nori on a bamboo sushi mat. Spread an even layer of sushi rice over the nori, leaving a 1-inch border at the top edge.
4 | Arrange the spicy tuna mixture, avocado slices, and julienned carrot horizontally across the middle of the rice.
5 | Roll the sushi tightly using the bamboo mat, applying gentle pressure to shape the roll.
6 | Lightly spray the outside of the roll with cooking spray and roll it in the panko breadcrumbs to coat.
7 | Place the roll in the air fryer basket. Cook for 8-10 minutes until the roll heats through and the breadcrumbs become crispy.
8 | Slice the roll into 8 pieces using a sharp knife.
9 | Repeat with the remaining nori, rice, spicy tuna, avocado, and carrot.
10 | Serve the spicy tuna crunch rolls with soy sauce, pickled ginger, and wasabi.

HONEY **MUSTARD SWORDFISH**

● **INGREDIENTS** 🥞 **YIELDS** | 4 SERVES

4 swordfish steaks
1/4 cup honey
2 tablespoons Dijon mustard
1 tablespoon olive oil

1 tablespoon fresh lemon juice
2 cloves garlic, minced
Salt and pepper to taste
Fresh parsley, chopped, for garnish

● **DIRECTIONS** ⏱ PREP TIME | 10 MIN 🍳 COOK TIME | 12 MIN

1 | Season the swordfish steaks with salt and pepper. Whisk together the honey, Dijon mustard, olive oil, lemon juice, and minced garlic in a small bowl.
2 | Brush the swordfish steaks with the honey-mustard mixture, ensuring they are well coated.
3 | Preheat the air fryer to 375°F (190°C).
4 | Place the swordfish steaks in the air fryer basket in a single layer. Cook for 10-12 minutes, turning halfway through, until the fish cooks through and the glaze caramelizes.
5 | Garnish with chopped fresh parsley before serving.

ITALIAN HERB-CRUSTED FLOUNDER

● INGREDIENTS 📚 YIELDS | 4 SERVES

4 flounder fillets
1/2 cup breadcrumbs
1/4 cup grated Parmesan cheese
2 tablespoons fresh parsley, chopped
1 tablespoon fresh basil, chopped

1 tablespoon fresh oregano, chopped
2 cloves garlic, minced
2 tablespoons olive oil
Salt and pepper to taste
Lemon wedges for serving

● DIRECTIONS ⏱ PREP TIME | 10 MIN 🍳 COOK TIME | 12 MIN

1 | Season the flounder fillets with salt and pepper. Mix the breadcrumbs, grated Parmesan cheese, fresh parsley, basil, oregano, minced garlic, and olive oil in a small bowl.

2 | Coat the flounder fillets with the herb mixture, pressing gently to adhere.

3 | Preheat the air fryer to 375°F (190°C).

4 | Place the coated flounder fillets in the air fryer basket in a single layer. Cook for 10-12 minutes or until the fish is golden and cooked through.

5 | Serve hot with lemon wedges.

PERFECT VEGGIES AND SIDES

ULTIMATE SWEET POTATO FRIES TRIO

● INGREDIENTS 🗐 YIELDS | 4 SERVES

For Classic Sweet Potato Fries:
2 large sweet potatoes, peeled and
cut into thin fries
2 tablespoons olive oil
1 teaspoon garlic powder
1 teaspoon paprika
Salt and pepper to taste

For Garlic Sweet Potato Fries:
2 large sweet potatoes, peeled and
cut into thin fries
2 tablespoons olive oil

2 teaspoons garlic powder
1 teaspoon sea salt
Fresh parsley, chopped (optional)

For Spicy Potato Fries:
2 large russet potatoes, peeled and
cut into thin fries
2 tablespoons vegetable oil
1 teaspoon cayenne pepper
1 teaspoon smoked paprika
Salt to taste

● DIRECTIONS ⏱ PREP TIME | 10 MIN 🍳 COOK TIME | 20 MIN

1 | Peel the sweet and russet potatoes, then cut them into thin fries.
2 | For Classic Sweet Potato Fries, toss the fries in a bowl with olive oil, garlic powder, paprika, salt, and pepper until evenly coated.
3 | For Garlic Sweet Potato Fries, toss the fries in a bowl with olive oil, garlic powder, and sea salt until evenly coated. Optionally, add fresh parsley.
4 | For Spicy Potato Fries, toss the fries in a bowl with vegetable oil, cayenne pepper, smoked paprika, and salt until evenly coated.
5 | Preheat the air fryer to 375°F (190°C).
6 | Arrange the fries in a single layer in the air fryer basket, cooking in batches if necessary. Cook for 15-20 minutes, shaking the basket halfway through, until the fries are crispy and golden brown.
7 | Serve immediately with your favorite dipping sauce.

CRISPY **ONION RINGS**

● INGREDIENTS   YIELDS | 4 SERVES

1 large onion, sliced into rings
1 cup buttermilk
1 cup all-purpose flour
1 teaspoon paprika

1 teaspoon garlic powder
Salt and pepper to taste
Cooking spray

● DIRECTIONS   PREP TIME | 15 MIN   COOK TIME | 12 MIN

1 | Soak the onion rings in buttermilk for at least 30 minutes, in a shallow dish, mix flour, paprika, garlic powder, salt, and pepper.
2 | Preheat the air fryer to 375°F (190°C).
3 | Dredge the onion rings in the flour mixture, coating well. Place the rings in the air fryer basket in a single layer. Lightly spray with cooking spray.
4 | Cook for 10-12 minutes, turning halfway through, until golden and crispy.
5 | Serve immediately with your favorite dipping sauce.

PARMESAN CRUSTED **CAULIFLOWER BITES**

● INGREDIENTS   YIELDS | 4 SERVES

1 head of cauliflower, cut into bite-sized pieces
1/2 cup grated Parmesan cheese
1/2 cup breadcrumbs

1 teaspoon garlic powder
1 teaspoon dried oregano
2 eggs, beaten
Salt and pepper to taste

● DIRECTIONS   PREP TIME | 15 MIN   COOK TIME | 15 MIN

1 | Blanch the cauliflower pieces in boiling water for 2 minutes, then immediately transfer them to an ice water bath to stop cooking. Drain well.
2 | Mix Parmesan cheese, breadcrumbs, garlic powder, oregano, salt, and pepper in a bowl.
3 | Dip the blanched cauliflower pieces into the beaten eggs, then coat with the breadcrumb mixture.
4 | Preheat the air fryer to 375°F (190°C).
5 | Place the cauliflower bites in a single layer in the air fryer basket, cooking in batches if necessary. Cook for 12-15 minutes, shaking the basket halfway through, until golden and crispy.
6 | Serve with marinara sauce or your favorite dipping sauce.

LEMON GARLIC **BROCCOLI CRUNCH**

INGREDIENTS YIELDS | 4 SERVES

1 head of broccoli, cut into florets
2 tablespoons olive oil
2 cloves garlic, minced

Zest and juice of 1 lemon
Salt and pepper to taste

DIRECTIONS PREP TIME | 10 MIN COOK TIME | 12 MIN

1 | Blanch the broccoli florets in boiling water for 2 minutes, then immediately transfer them to an ice water bath to stop cooking. Drain well.
2 | Toss the blanched broccoli florets in a large bowl with olive oil, minced garlic, lemon zest, lemon juice, salt, and pepper until evenly coated.
3 | Preheat the air fryer to 375°F (190°C).
4 | Place the broccoli in a single layer in the air fryer basket. Cook for 10-12 minutes, shaking the basket halfway through, until the broccoli is tender and slightly crispy. Serve warm.

CARAMELIZED **RED CABBAGE**

INGREDIENTS YIELDS | 4 SERVES

1 large head of red cabbage, cut into 1-inch thick steaks
3 tablespoons olive oil
3 tablespoons balsamic vinegar
2 tablespoons brown sugar

2 cloves garlic, minced
Salt and pepper to taste
Fresh parsley, chopped (optional, for garnish)

DIRECTIONS PREP TIME | 10 MIN COOK TIME | 30 MIN

1 | Preheat the air fryer to 375°F (190°C).
2 | In a small bowl, mix the olive oil, balsamic vinegar, brown sugar, minced garlic, salt, and pepper.
3 | Brush both sides of each cabbage steak with the balsamic mixture, ensuring they are well coated.
4 | Place the cabbage steaks in a single layer in the air fryer basket. Cook for 25-30 minutes, flipping halfway through, until the cabbage is tender and caramelized.
5 | Remove from the air fryer and let it cool slightly before serving.
6 | Garnish with chopped fresh parsley if desired, and serve warm.

LEMON ROASTED ASPARAGUS

● INGREDIENTS YIELDS | 4 SERVES

1 bunch of asparagus, trimmed
2 tablespoons olive oil
Zest and juice of 1 lemon

2 cloves garlic, minced
Salt and pepper to taste

● DIRECTIONS PREP TIME | 10 MIN COOK TIME | 12 MIN

1 | Trim the tough ends of the asparagus. Optionally, peel the lower part of the stalks.
2 | Place the asparagus in boiling water to blanch it for 1-2 minutes, then quickly transfer to an ice bath. Drain and pat dry.
3 | Toss the blanched asparagus in a large bowl with olive oil, lemon zest, lemon juice, minced garlic, salt, and pepper until evenly coated.
4 | Preheat the air fryer to 375°F (190°C).
5 | Place the asparagus in a single layer in the air fryer basket. Cook for 10-12 minutes, shaking the basket halfway through, until the asparagus is tender and slightly crispy. Serve warm.

SEA SALT SPINACH CHIPS

● INGREDIENTS YIELDS | 4 SERVES

4 cups fresh spinach leaves, washed
and thoroughly dried

1 tablespoon olive oil
1 teaspoon sea salt

● DIRECTIONS PREP TIME | 5 MIN COOK TIME | 7 MIN

1 | Wash and thoroughly dry the spinach leaves. Toss the spinach in a large bowl with olive oil and sea salt until evenly coated. **2 |** Preheat the air fryer to 375°F (190°C).
3 | Place the spinach leaves in a single layer in the air fryer basket. Cook for 5-7 minutes, shaking the basket halfway through, until the spinach leaves are crispy.
4 | Serve immediately as a healthy snack.

ROSEMARY **BABY POTATOES**

INGREDIENTS — YIELDS | 4 SERVES

1 pound baby potatoes, halved
2 tablespoons olive oil
2 teaspoons fresh rosemary, chopped
(or 1 teaspoon dried rosemary)

2 cloves garlic, minced
Salt and pepper to taste

DIRECTIONS — PREP TIME | 10 MIN — COOK TIME | 20 MIN

1 | Toss the baby potatoes in a large bowl with olive oil, rosemary, minced garlic, salt, and pepper until evenly coated.
2 | Preheat the air fryer to 375°F (190°C).
3 | Place the potatoes in a single layer in the air fryer basket. Cook for 15-20 minutes, shaking the basket halfway through, until the potatoes are tender and golden brown. Serve warm.

RAINBOW **VEGGIE SKEWERS**

INGREDIENTS — YIELDS | 4 SERVES

1 red bell pepper, cut into chunks
1 yellow bell pepper, cut into chunks
1 green bell pepper, cut into chunks
1 red onion, cut into chunks
1 zucchini, sliced into thick rounds
1 cup cherry tomatoes

2 tablespoons olive oil
1 teaspoon dried oregano
1 teaspoon garlic powder
Salt and pepper to taste
Wooden or metal skewers

DIRECTIONS — PREP TIME | 15 MIN — COOK TIME | 12 MIN

1 | If using wooden skewers, soak them in water for at least 30 minutes to prevent burning.
2 | Toss the bell peppers, red onion, zucchini, and cherry tomatoes in a large bowl with olive oil, dried oregano, garlic powder, salt, and pepper until evenly coated.
3 | Thread the vegetables onto the skewers, alternating colors to create a rainbow effect.
4 | Preheat the air fryer to 375°F (190°C).
5 | Place the skewers in a single layer in the air fryer basket. Cook for 10-12 minutes, turning halfway through, until the vegetables are tender and slightly charred. Serve warm.

GARLIC GREEN **BEAN SIZZLERS**

● INGREDIENTS   YIELDS | 4 SERVES

1 pound fresh green beans, trimmed
2 tablespoons olive oil
3 cloves garlic, minced

Salt and pepper to taste
Lemon wedges for serving (optional)

● DIRECTIONS   PREP TIME | 5 MIN   COOK TIME | 10 MIN

1 | Toss the green beans in a large bowl with olive oil, minced garlic, salt, and pepper until evenly coated.
2 | Preheat the air fryer to 375°F (190°C).
3 | Place the green beans in a single layer in the air fryer basket. Cook for 8-10 minutes, shaking the basket halfway through, until the green beans are tender and slightly crispy.
4 | Serve warm, with lemon wedges on the side if desired.

STUFFED CREAM **CHEESE MUSHROOMS**

● INGREDIENTS   YIELDS | 4 SERVES

16 large button mushrooms, stems removed
8 ounces cream cheese, softened
1/4 cup grated Parmesan cheese

2 cloves garlic, minced
2 tablespoons chopped fresh parsley
Salt and pepper to taste
Cooking spray

● DIRECTIONS   PREP TIME | 15 MIN   COOK TIME | 12 MIN

1 | Mix the cream cheese, Parmesan cheese, minced garlic, chopped parsley, salt, and pepper in a bowl until well combined.
2 | Fill each mushroom cap with the cream cheese mixture.
3 | Preheat the air fryer to 375°F (190°C).
4 | Lightly spray the air fryer basket with cooking spray. Place the stuffed mushrooms in a single layer in the basket.
5 | Cook for 10-12 minutes, until the mushrooms are tender and the filling is golden and bubbly. Serve warm.

CHEESY **CAULIFLOWER BALLS**

● **INGREDIENTS** ⊜ YIELDS | 4 SERVES

1 head of cauliflower, cut into florets
1 cup shredded cheddar cheese
1/2 cup breadcrumbs
1/4 cup grated Parmesan cheese
2 cloves garlic, minced

2 eggs, beaten
1 teaspoon dried oregano
Salt and pepper to taste
Cooking spray

● **DIRECTIONS** ⏱ PREP TIME | 15 MIN 🍳 COOK TIME | 15 MIN

1 | Blanch the cauliflower florets in boiling water for 2 minutes, then immediately transfer them to an ice water bath to stop cooking. Drain well and finely chop.
2 | Combine the chopped cauliflower, shredded cheddar cheese, breadcrumbs, grated Parmesan cheese, minced garlic, beaten eggs, dried oregano, salt, and pepper in a large bowl. Mix until well combined.
3 | Form the mixture into small balls about the size of a golf ball.
4 | Preheat the air fryer to 375°F (190°C).
5 | Lightly spray the air fryer basket with cooking spray. Place the cauliflower balls in a single layer in the basket.
6 | Cook for 12-15 minutes, shaking the basket halfway through, until the balls are golden brown and crispy.
7 | Serve warm with your favorite dipping sauce.

PARMESAN **ZUCCHINI STICKS**

● **INGREDIENTS** ⊜ YIELDS | 4 SERVES

2 medium zucchinis, cut into sticks
1/2 cup grated Parmesan cheese
1/2 cup breadcrumbs
1 teaspoon garlic powder

1 teaspoon dried oregano
2 eggs, beaten
Salt and pepper to taste
Cooking spray

● **DIRECTIONS** ⏱ PREP TIME | 10 MIN 🍳 COOK TIME | 12 MIN

1 | Mix Parmesan cheese, breadcrumbs, garlic powder, dried oregano, salt, and pepper in a bowl.
2 | Dip the zucchini sticks into the beaten eggs, then coat with the breadcrumb mixture.
3 | Preheat the air fryer to 375°F (190°C).
4 | Lightly spray the air fryer basket with cooking spray. Place the zucchini sticks in a single layer in the basket.
5 | Cook for 10-12 minutes, shaking the basket halfway through, until the zucchini sticks are golden brown and crispy.
6 | Serve warm with your favorite dipping sauce.

ZUCCHINI FRITTERS

● INGREDIENTS 🍽 YIELDS | 4 SERVES

2 medium zucchinis, grated
1/2 cup all-purpose flour
1/4 cup grated Parmesan cheese
1/4 cup chopped green onions
1 large egg, beaten

2 cloves garlic, minced
1 teaspoon salt
1/2 teaspoon black pepper
Cooking spray

● DIRECTIONS ⏱ PREP TIME | 15 MIN 🍳 COOK TIME | 12 MIN

1 | Grate the zucchinis and place them in a colander. Sprinkle with salt and let sit for 10 minutes to draw out moisture. Then, squeeze out excess moisture using a clean kitchen towel or paper towel.
2 | Combine the grated zucchini, flour, Parmesan cheese, green onions, beaten egg, minced garlic, salt, and black pepper in a large bowl. Mix until well combined.
3 | Form the mixture into small patties or fritters.
4 | Preheat the air fryer to 375°F (190°C).
5 | Lightly spray the air fryer basket with cooking spray. Place the zucchini fritters in a single layer in the basket.
6 | Cook for 10-12 minutes, flipping halfway through, until the fritters are golden brown and crispy.
7 | Serve warm with your favorite dipping sauce.

GARLIC ROASTED EGGPLANT

● INGREDIENTS 🍽 YIELDS | 4 SERVES

1 large eggplant, cut into bite-sized
pieces
2 tablespoons olive oil
3 cloves garlic, minced

1 teaspoon dried oregano
Salt and pepper to taste
Fresh parsley, chopped (optional)

● DIRECTIONS ⏱ PREP TIME | 10 MIN 🍳 COOK TIME | 12 MIN

1 | Toss the eggplant pieces in a large bowl with olive oil, minced garlic, dried oregano, salt, and pepper until evenly coated.
2 | Preheat the air fryer to 375°F (190°C).
3 | Place the eggplant in a single layer in the air fryer basket. Cook for 15-20 minutes, shaking the basket halfway through, until tender and golden brown.
4 | Garnish with fresh parsley if desired, and serve warm.

CHEESY **POTATO CROQUETTES**

● **INGREDIENTS** 🥞 **YIELDS** | 4 SERVES

2 cups mashed potatoes
1 cup shredded cheddar cheese
1/2 cup breadcrumbs
1/4 cup grated Parmesan cheese
1/4 cup chopped green onions

1 large egg, beaten
2 cloves garlic, minced
Salt and pepper to taste
Cooking spray

● **DIRECTIONS** ⏱ PREP TIME | 20 MIN 🍳 COOK TIME | 12 MIN

1 | Combine mashed potatoes, shredded cheddar cheese, breadcrumbs, grated Parmesan cheese, chopped green onions, beaten egg, minced garlic, salt, and pepper in a large bowl. Mix until well combined.
2 | Form the mixture into small balls or croquette shapes.
3 | Preheat the air fryer to 375°F (190°C).
4 | Lightly spray the air fryer basket with cooking spray. Place the potato croquettes in a single layer in the basket.
5 | Cook for 10-12 minutes, shaking the basket halfway through, until the croquettes are golden brown and crispy.
6 | Serve warm with your favorite dipping sauce.

GRILLED **MEXICAN CORN**

● **INGREDIENTS** 🥞 **YIELDS** | 4 SERVES

4 ears of corn, husked
2 tablespoons olive oil
1/2 cup mayonnaise
1/2 cup crumbled Cotija cheese (or feta cheese)

1 teaspoon chili powder
1 tablespoon fresh cilantro, chopped
1 lime, cut into wedges
Salt to taste

● **DIRECTIONS** ⏱ PREP TIME | 10 MIN 🍳 COOK TIME | 12 MIN

1 | Brush the corn with olive oil and season with salt.
2 | Preheat the air fryer to 375°F (190°C).
3 | Place the corn in a single layer in the air fryer basket. Cook for 10-12 minutes, turning the corn halfway through, until tender and slightly charred.
4 | While the corn is cooking, mix the mayonnaise, crumbled Cotija cheese, and chili powder in a bowl.
5 | Once you cook the corn, spread the mayonnaise mixture over each ear of corn.
6 | Sprinkle with chopped cilantro and serve with lime wedges.

SOY-GLAZED **MUSHROOMS**

● INGREDIENTS 🍳 YIELDS | 4 SERVES

1 pound button or cremini mushrooms, cleaned and halved
2 tablespoons soy sauce
1 tablespoon olive oil
1 tablespoon honey
2 cloves garlic, minced

1 teaspoon sesame oil
1 teaspoon rice vinegar
1 tablespoon sesame seeds
Chopped green onions for garnish (optional)

● DIRECTIONS ⏱ PREP TIME | 10 MIN 🍳 COOK TIME | 12 MIN

1 | Mix a bowl of soy sauce, olive oil, honey, minced garlic, sesame oil, and rice vinegar.
2 | Toss the mushrooms in the soy glaze mixture until evenly coated.
3 | Preheat the air fryer to 375°F (190°C).
4 | Place the mushrooms in a single layer in the air fryer basket. Cook for 10-12 minutes, shaking the basket halfway through, until the mushrooms are tender and caramelized.
5 | Sprinkle with sesame seeds and garnish with chopped green onions if desired. Serve warm.

PARMESAN **BROCCOLI STEAKS**

● INGREDIENTS 🍳 YIELDS | 4 SERVES

2 large heads of broccoli sliced into thick steaks
2 tablespoons olive oil
1/2 cup grated Parmesan cheese

1 teaspoon garlic powder
1 teaspoon dried oregano
Salt and pepper to taste
Lemon wedges for serving (optional)

● DIRECTIONS ⏱ PREP TIME | 10 MIN 🍳 COOK TIME | 12 MIN

1 | Blanch the broccoli steaks in boiling water for 2 minutes, then immediately transfer them to an ice water bath to stop cooking. Drain well and pat dry.
2 | Mix olive oil, grated Parmesan cheese, garlic powder, dried oregano, salt, and pepper in a bowl.
3 | Brush the broccoli steaks with the olive oil and Parmesan mixture until evenly coated.
4 | Preheat the air fryer to 375°F (190°C).
5 | Place the broccoli steaks in a single layer in the air fryer basket. Cook for 10-12 minutes, shaking the basket halfway through, until the broccoli is tender and the Parmesan coating is golden and crispy.
6 | Serve warm with lemon wedges on the side if desired.

CAULIFLOWER AND **BROCCOLI PATTIES**

● **INGREDIENTS** 📖 YIELDS | 4 SERVES

1 head of cauliflower, cut into florets
1 head of broccoli, cut into florets
1/2 cup grated Parmesan cheese
1/2 cup breadcrumbs
2 cloves garlic, minced

1/4 cup chopped green onions
2 large eggs, beaten
1 teaspoon dried oregano
Salt and pepper to taste
Cooking spray

● **DIRECTIONS** ⏱ PREP TIME | 15 MIN 🍳 COOK TIME | 12 MIN

1 | Blanch the cauliflower and broccoli florets in boiling water for 2 minutes, then immediately transfer them to an ice water bath to stop the cooking process. Drain well and finely chop.
2 | In a large bowl, combine the chopped cauliflower and broccoli, grated Parmesan cheese, breadcrumbs, minced garlic, chopped green onions, beaten eggs, dried oregano, salt, and pepper. Mix until well combined.
3 | Form the mixture into small patties.
4 | Preheat the air fryer to 375°F (190°C).
5 | Lightly spray the air fryer basket with cooking spray. Place the patties in a single layer in the basket.
6 | Cook for 10-12 minutes, flipping halfway through, until the patties are golden brown and crispy.
7 | Serve warm with your favorite dipping sauce.

TWICE-BAKED **POTATOES**

● **INGREDIENTS** 📖 YIELDS | 4 SERVES

4 medium russet potatoes
1/2 cup sour cream
1/4 cup unsalted butter, melted
1/2 cup shredded cheddar cheese

1/4 cup chopped green onions
1/4 cup cooked and crumbled bacon
Salt and pepper to taste
Cooking spray

● **DIRECTIONS** ⏱ PREP TIME | 15 MIN 🍳 COOK TIME | 30 MIN

1 | Preheat the air fryer to 400°F (200°C) for about 5 minutes.
2 | Wash and dry the potatoes. Pierce each potato a few times with a fork.
3 | Lightly spray the potatoes with cooking spray and place them in the air fryer basket.
4 | Cook the potatoes at 400°F (200°C) for 20-25 minutes or until tender and easily pierced with a fork.
5 | Remove the potatoes from the air fryer and let them cool slightly. Cut each potato in half lengthwise and scoop out most of the flesh, leaving a small border to create a sturdy shell.
6 | In a bowl, mash the scooped-out potato flesh with sour cream, melted butter, shredded cheddar cheese, chopped green onions, cooked bacon, salt, and pepper until well combined.
7 | Fill each potato shell with the mashed potato mixture, dividing it evenly among the shells.
8 | Place the stuffed potatoes back in the air fryer basket.
9 | Cook at 375°F (190°C) for 5-7 minutes or until the tops are golden brown and the filling is heated.
10 | Remove from the air fryer and let cool slightly before serving.

SPICED **VEGGIE COUSCOUS**

 INGREDIENTS YIELDS | 4 SERVES

1 cup couscous
1 1/4 cups vegetable broth or water
1 cup mixed vegetables (such as bell peppers, carrots, zucchini), diced
2 tablespoons olive oil
1 teaspoon ground cumin
1 teaspoon ground coriander

1/2 teaspoon ground cinnamon
1/2 teaspoon ground turmeric
1/2 teaspoon paprika
Salt and pepper to taste
Fresh cilantro, chopped (optional)
Lemon wedges for serving (optional)

DIRECTIONS PREP TIME | 10 MIN COOK TIME | 12 MIN

1 | In a pot, bring the vegetable broth or water to a boil. Remove from heat, add the couscous, cover, and let sit for 5 minutes—fluff with a fork and set aside.
2 | Toss the mixed vegetables in a large bowl with olive oil, ground cumin, coriander, cinnamon, turmeric, paprika, salt, and pepper until evenly coated.
3 | Preheat the air fryer to 375°F (190°C).
4 | Place the spiced vegetables in a single layer in the air fryer basket. Cook for 10-12 minutes, shaking the basket halfway through, until the vegetables are tender and slightly crispy.
5 | In a large bowl, combine the cooked couscous with the air-fried vegetables. Mix well.
6 | Garnish with chopped fresh cilantro and serve with lemon wedges if desired.

BACON-WRAPPED **ASPARAGUS**

 INGREDIENTS YIELDS | 4 SERVES

1 bunch asparagus, trimmed
8 slices bacon
2 tablespoons olive oil

1 teaspoon garlic powder
1 teaspoon black pepper
Lemon wedges for serving (optional)

DIRECTIONS PREP TIME | 10 MIN COOK TIME | 12 MIN

1 | Toss the asparagus spears in a large bowl with olive oil, garlic powder, and black pepper until evenly coated.
2 | Preheat the air fryer to 375°F (190°C).
3 | Wrap each asparagus spear with a slice of bacon, starting at the bottom and spiraling up to the top.
4 | Place the bacon-wrapped asparagus in a single layer in the air fryer basket.
5 | Cook for 10-12 minutes, turning halfway through, until the bacon is crispy and the asparagus is tender.
6 | Serve warm with lemon wedges on the side if desired.

CRISPY **TOFU BITES**

● **INGREDIENTS**   ▦ **YIELDS | 4 SERVES**

1 block (14 ounces) firm tofu, pressed
and cut into 1-inch cubes
1/2 cup cornstarch
1/2 cup breadcrumbs
1 teaspoon garlic powder
1 teaspoon onion powder
Salt and pepper to taste
Cooking spray

Sweet and Sour Sauce:
1/4 cup rice vinegar
1/4 cup ketchup
1/4 cup brown sugar
1 tablespoon soy sauce
1 tablespoon cornstarch mixed with 2
tablespoons water

● **DIRECTIONS**   ⏱ **PREP TIME | 15 MIN**   ▣ **COOK TIME | 15 MIN**

1 | Preheat the air fryer to 375°F (190°C).
2 | Combine the cornstarch, breadcrumbs, garlic powder, onion powder, salt, and pepper in a
bowl.
3 | Toss the tofu cubes in the cornstarch mixture until evenly coated.
4 | Lightly spray the air fryer basket with cooking spray. Place the tofu nuggets in a single layer in
the basket.
5 | Cook for 12-15 minutes, shaking the basket halfway through, until the tofu nuggets are golden
brown and crispy.
6 | While the tofu is cooking, prepare the sweet and sour sauce. Combine rice vinegar, ketchup,
brown sugar, and soy sauce in a small saucepan. Bring to a simmer over medium heat.
7 | Stir in the cornstarch mixture and cook until the sauce thickens about 1-2 minutes.
8 | Serve the crispy tofu nuggets with the sweet and sour sauce on the side for dipping.

HONEY GLAZED **CARROT DELIGHT**

● **INGREDIENTS**   ▦ **YIELDS | 4 SERVES**

4 large carrots, peeled and cut into
sticks
2 tablespoons honey

1 tablespoon olive oil
1/2 teaspoon ground cinnamon
Salt to taste

● **DIRECTIONS**   ⏱ **PREP TIME | 10 MIN**   ▣ **COOK TIME | 15 MIN**

1 | Peel the carrots and cut them into sticks. Toss the carrot sticks in a large bowl with honey, olive
oil, ground cinnamon, and salt until evenly coated.
2 | Preheat the air fryer to 375°F (190°C).
3 | Place the carrot sticks in a single layer in the air fryer basket. Cook for 12-15 minutes, shaking
the basket halfway through, until tender and caramelized. Serve warm

MOROCCAN **FALAFEL BITES**

● INGREDIENTS  YIELDS | 4 SERVES

1 can (15 ounces) chickpeas, drained and rinsed
1 small onion, finely chopped
3 cloves garlic, minced
1/4 cup fresh parsley, chopped
1/4 cup fresh cilantro, chopped
1 teaspoon ground cumin
1 teaspoon ground coriander
1/2 teaspoon ground cinnamon
1/2 teaspoon ground turmeric
1/4 teaspoon cayenne pepper (optional)

1/4 cup all-purpose flour
Salt and pepper to taste
Cooking spray
Tahini Dressing:
1/4 cup tahini
2 tablespoons lemon juice
1 tablespoon olive oil
1 clove garlic, minced
2-3 tablespoons water (to thin the dressing)
Salt to taste

● DIRECTIONS  PREP TIME | 20 MIN  COOK TIME | 12 MIN

1 | In a food processor, combine the chickpeas, chopped onion, minced garlic, fresh parsley, fresh cilantro, ground cumin, ground coriander, ground cinnamon, ground turmeric, cayenne pepper (if using), all-purpose flour, salt, and pepper. Pulse until the mixture is well combined and slightly chunky.
2 | Form the mixture into small balls about the size of a golf ball.
3 | Preheat the air fryer to 375°F (190°C).
4 | Lightly spray the air fryer basket with cooking spray. Place the falafel balls in a single layer in the basket.
5 | Cook for 10-12 minutes, shaking the basket halfway through, until the falafel balls are golden brown and crispy.
6 | While the falafel is cooking, prepare the tahini dressing. In a small bowl, whisk together tahini, lemon juice, olive oil, minced garlic, and enough water to reach the desired consistency—season with salt to taste.
7 | For dipping, serve the Moroccan falafel balls warm with the tahini dressing on the side.

HONEY NUT **BRUSSELS SPROUTS**

● INGREDIENTS  YIELDS | 4 SERVES

1 pound Brussels sprouts, trimmed and halved
2 tablespoons olive oil

2 tablespoons honey
1/4 cup chopped walnuts or pecans
Salt and pepper to taste

● DIRECTIONS  PREP TIME | 10 MIN  COOK TIME | 20 MIN

1 | Toss the Brussels sprouts in a large bowl with olive oil, honey, chopped walnuts or pecans, salt, and pepper until evenly coated.
2 | Preheat the air fryer to 375°F (190°C).
3 | Place the Brussels sprouts in a single layer in the air fryer basket. Cook for 15-20 minutes, shaking the basket halfway through, until the Brussels sprouts are tender and caramelized. Serve warm.

LOADED **SWEET POTATO BOATS**

● **INGREDIENTS** 🍳 YIELDS | 4 SERVES

2 large sweet potatoes
1 cup black beans, drained and rinsed
1/2 cup corn kernels (fresh, canned, or frozen)
1/2 cup diced tomatoes
1/2 cup shredded cheddar cheese
1/4 cup sour cream

1/4 cup chopped green onions
1/4 cup chopped fresh cilantro
1 tablespoon olive oil
1 teaspoon ground cumin
1/2 teaspoon smoked paprika
Salt and pepper to taste
Cooking spray

● **DIRECTIONS** ⏱ PREP TIME | 10 MIN 📟 COOK TIME | 20 MIN

1 | Preheat the air fryer to 375°F (190°C) for about 5 minutes.
2 | Wash and dry the sweet potatoes. Cut them in half lengthwise and brush with olive oil. Season with salt, pepper, cumin, and smoked paprika.
3 | Lightly spray the air fryer basket with cooking spray. Place the sweet potato halves in the basket, cut side up.
4 | Cook in the air fryer at 375°F (190°C) for 20 minutes or until the sweet potatoes are tender and cooked.
5 | Remove the sweet potatoes from the air fryer and let them cool slightly. Scoop out some flesh to create a boat shape, leaving a small border around the edges.
6 | Mix the black beans, corn, diced tomatoes, and a pinch of salt and pepper in a bowl. Fill the sweet potato boats with this mixture and top with shredded cheddar cheese.
7 | Put the stuffed sweet potatoes back in the air fryer and cook at 375°F (190°C) for 5 minutes until the cheese melts and turns bubbly.
8 | Remove from the air fryer and garnish with sour cream, chopped green onions, and fresh cilantro before serving.

CINNAMON SWEET **POTATO STICKS**

● **INGREDIENTS** 🍳 YIELDS | 4 SERVES

2 large sweet potatoes, peeled and cut into sticks
2 tablespoons olive oil

1 teaspoon ground cinnamon
1 tablespoon brown sugar
Pinch of salt

● **DIRECTIONS** ⏱ PREP TIME | 10 MIN 📟 COOK TIME | 20 MIN

1 | Peel the sweet potatoes and cut them into sticks. Toss the sticks in a large bowl with olive oil, ground cinnamon, brown sugar, and a pinch of salt until evenly coated.
2 | Preheat the air fryer to 375°F (190°C).
3 | Arrange the sticks in a single layer in the air fryer basket, cooking in batches if necessary. Cook for 15-20 minutes, shaking the basket halfway through, until the sticks are crispy and golden. Serve warm.

CHAPTER 7

QUICK BITES & APPETIZERS

VARIETY **SLIDERS TRIO**

● **INGREDIENTS** 🍽 YIELDS | 4 SERVINGS OF EACH TYPE

For Beef Sliders:
1 lb ground beef
1/2 teaspoon salt
1/4 teaspoon black pepper
4 slider buns
Sliced cheese (optional)
Lettuce, tomato, pickles (optional)
For BBQ Chicken Sliders:
1 lb ground chicken
1/4 cup BBQ sauce
1/2 teaspoon salt
1/4 teaspoon black pepper
4 slider buns
Coleslaw (optional)

For Veggie Sliders:
1 can (15 oz) black beans, drained and
rinsed
1/2 cup breadcrumbs
1/4 cup diced onion
1/4 cup shredded carrot
1 teaspoon cumin
1/2 teaspoon garlic powder
1/2 teaspoon chili powder
4 slider buns
Avocado slices, lettuce, tomato
(optional)
For All:
Cooking spray

● **DIRECTIONS** ⏱ PREP TIME | 15 MIN 🍳 COOK TIME | 12 MIN

1 | Beef Sliders:
In a bowl, mix ground beef, salt, and black pepper. Form into 4 patties. Preheat the air fryer to 375°F (190°C). Lightly spray the air fryer basket with cooking spray and place the patties inside. Cook for 10-12 minutes, flipping halfway through, until the internal temperature reaches 160°F (71°C). Assemble with slider buns and desired toppings.

2 | BBQ Chicken Sliders:
Mix ground chicken, BBQ sauce, salt, and black pepper in a bowl. Form into 4 patties. Preheat the air fryer to 375°F (190°C). Lightly spray the air fryer basket with cooking spray and place the patties inside. Cook for 10-12 minutes, flipping halfway through, until the internal temperature reaches 165°F (74°C). Assemble with slider buns and coleslaw.

3 | Veggie Sliders:
In a bowl, mash black beans with a fork. Add breadcrumbs, diced onion, shredded carrot, cumin, garlic powder, and chili powder. Mix well and form into 4 patties. Preheat the air fryer to 375°F (190°C). Lightly spray the air fryer basket with cooking spray and place the patties inside. Cook for 10-12 minutes, flipping halfway through, until crispy. Assemble with slider buns and desired toppings.

VARIETY POPCORN BITES

● INGREDIENTS  YIELDS | 4 SERVES

Shrimp Popcorn:
1 pound large shrimp, peeled and deveined
1 cup buttermilk
1 cup all-purpose flour
1 teaspoon paprika
1/2 teaspoon garlic powder
1/2 teaspoon salt
1/2 teaspoon black pepper
Cooking spray

Zucchini Popcorn:
2 medium zucchinis, cut into bite-sized pieces
1 cup buttermilk
1 cup panko breadcrumbs
1/2 teaspoon paprika
1/2 teaspoon garlic powder
1/2 teaspoon salt
1/2 teaspoon black pepper
Cooking spray

● DIRECTIONS ⏱ PREP TIME | 10 MIN 🍳 COOK TIME | 15 MIN

1 | Preheat the air fryer to 375°F (190°C) for about 5 minutes.

2 | For Shrimp Popcorn:
In a bowl, soak the shrimp in buttermilk for 5 minutes. Mix the flour, paprika, garlic powder, salt, and black pepper in another bowl. Remove the shrimp from the buttermilk, letting the excess drip off, and dredge in the flour mixture, coating evenly. Lightly spray the air fryer basket with cooking spray. Place the shrimp in a single layer in the air fryer basket. Cook for 8-10 minutes, shaking the basket halfway through, until the shrimp are golden and crispy.

3 | For Zucchini Popcorn:
In a bowl, soak the zucchini pieces in buttermilk for 5 minutes. Mix the panko breadcrumbs, paprika, garlic powder, salt, and black pepper in another bowl. Remove the zucchini pieces from the buttermilk, letting the excess drip off, and dredge in the panko mixture, coating evenly. Lightly spray the air fryer basket with cooking spray. Place the zucchini pieces in a single layer in the air fryer basket. Cook for 10-12 minutes, shaking the basket halfway through, until the zucchini pieces are golden and crispy. **4 |** Serve the Variety Popcorn Bites hot with your favorite dipping sauces.

CHICKEN POPCORN

● INGREDIENTS 🥞 YIELDS | 4 SERVES

1 pound boneless, skinless chicken breasts cut into bite-sized pieces
1 cup buttermilk
1 cup panko breadcrumbs
1/2 cup all-purpose flour

1 teaspoon paprika
1/2 teaspoon garlic powder
1/2 teaspoon salt
1/2 teaspoon black pepper
Cooking spray

● DIRECTIONS ⏱ PREP TIME | 15 MIN 🍳 COOK TIME | 12 MIN

1 | Preheat the air fryer to 375°F (190°C). **2 |** Soak the chicken pieces in buttermilk for at least 15 minutes. **3 |** Mix the panko breadcrumbs, flour, paprika, garlic powder, salt, and black pepper in a shallow bowl. **4 |** Dredge the buttermilk-soaked chicken pieces in the breadcrumb mixture, ensuring they are well coated. **5 |** Lightly spray the air fryer basket with cooking spray. Place the chicken pieces in a single layer in the basket. **6 |** Cook for 10-12 minutes, shaking the basket halfway through, until the chicken is golden brown and crispy. **7 |** Serve warm with your favorite dipping sauce.

VARIETY MINI PIZZAS

● INGREDIENTS   🍽 YIELDS | 6 MINI PIZZAS (1 OF EACH TYPE)

6 mini pizza crusts or English muffins, halved
1 cup pizza sauce
2 cups shredded mozzarella cheese
Cooking spray

For Pepperoni Mini Pizza:
1/2 cup sliced pepperoni

For Margherita Mini Pizza:
1/2 cup sliced fresh mozzarella
1/4 cup fresh basil leaves, torn

For Hawaiian Mini Pizza:
1/4 cup diced ham
1/4 cup pineapple tidbits

For BBQ Chicken Mini Pizza:
1/2 cup cooked chicken, shredded
1/4 cup BBQ sauce
1/4 cup red onion, thinly sliced

For Veggie Lovers Mini Pizza:
1/4 cup bell peppers, diced
1/4 cup black olives, sliced
1/4 cup mushrooms, sliced

For Buffalo Chicken Mini Pizza:
1/2 cup cooked chicken, shredded
1/4 cup Buffalo sauce
1/4 cup blue cheese crumbles

● DIRECTIONS   ⏱ PREP TIME | 15 MIN   🔲 COOK TIME | 10 MIN

1 | Preheat the air fryer to 375°F (190°C).

2 | Lightly spray the air fryer basket with cooking spray. Place mini pizza crusts or English muffin halves in the basket, cut side up.

3 | Spread pizza sauce evenly over each crust or muffin half.

4 | Sprinkle shredded mozzarella cheese over the sauce on each pizza.

5 | *For Pepperoni Mini Pizza:*
Top with sliced pepperoni.

6 | *For Margherita Mini Pizza:*
Top with sliced fresh mozzarella and torn basil leaves.

7 | *For BBQ Chicken Mini Pizza:*
Mix shredded chicken with BBQ sauce. Top each pizza with BBQ chicken mixture and sliced red onions.

8 | *For Veggie Lovers Mini Pizza:*
Top with diced bell peppers, sliced black olives, and sliced mushrooms.

9 | *For Hawaiian Mini Pizza:*
Top with diced ham and pineapple tidbits.

10 | *For Buffalo Chicken Mini Pizza:*
Mix shredded chicken with Buffalo sauce. Top each pizza with Buffalo chicken mixture and blue cheese crumbles.

11 | Cook in the air fryer for 8-10 minutes until the cheese melts and becomes bubbly, and the crust turns crispy.

VARIETY **DEEP-FRIED SANDWICHES**

● **INGREDIENTS** 🍽 **YIELDS | 6 SANDWICHES (2 OF EACH TYPE)**

12 slices of white bread (2 slices per sandwich)
3 large eggs
1/2 cup milk
1/2 cup all-purpose flour
Cooking spray
For Deep-Fried Monte Cristo Sandwich:
2 slices of ham
2 slices of turkey
2 slices of Swiss cheese
Powdered sugar and raspberry jam for serving

For Deep-Fried Buffalo Chicken Sandwich:
1 cup cooked chicken, shredded
1/4 cup Buffalo sauce
2 slices of cheddar cheese
For Deep-Fried BBQ Pulled Pork Sandwich:
1 cup cooked pulled pork
1/4 cup BBQ sauce
2 slices of coleslaw

● **DIRECTIONS** ⏱ **PREP TIME | 20 MIN** 🍳 **COOK TIME | 10 MIN**

1 | Preheat the air fryer to 375°F (190°C).

2 | Lightly spray the air fryer basket with cooking spray. Whisk together the eggs and milk in a bowl. Place the flour in a separate bowl.

3 | Dip the bread slices in the egg mixture for each sandwich, then coat with flour.

4 | *Monte Cristo Sandwich:*

Layer ham, turkey, and Swiss cheese between two prepared bread slices. Dip the assembled sandwich into the egg mixture again and coat with flour. Spray with cooking spray.

5 | *Buffalo Chicken Sandwich:*

Mix shredded chicken with Buffalo sauce. Layer the Buffalo chicken and cheddar cheese between two slices of prepared bread. Dip the assembled sandwich into the egg mixture again and coat with flour. Spray with cooking spray.

6 | *BBQ Pulled Pork Sandwich:*

Mix pulled pork with BBQ sauce. Layer the BBQ-pulled pork and coleslaw between two slices of prepared bread. Dip the assembled sandwich into the egg mixture again and coat with flour. Spray with cooking spray.

7 | Place the sandwiches in the air fryer basket. Cook for 8-10 minutes, flipping halfway through, until golden brown and crispy.

8 | *Monte Cristo Sandwich:*

Sprinkle with powdered sugar and serve with raspberry jam.

LOADED **NACHOS**

● INGREDIENTS 📋 YIELDS | 4 SERVES

Base Nachos:
8 cups tortilla chips
2 cups shredded cheddar cheese
1 cup shredded Monterey Jack cheese
Classic Cheese Nachos:
1 cup salsa
1/2 cup sliced black olives
1/2 cup sliced jalapeños
1/4 cup sour cream
1/4 cup chopped fresh cilantro

BBQ Chicken Nachos:
1 cup cooked chicken, shredded
1/2 cup BBQ sauce
1/4 cup sliced red onions
1/4 cup chopped fresh cilantro
Loaded Veggie Nachos:
1/2 cup diced bell peppers
1/2 cup diced tomatoes
1/2 cup corn kernels
1/4 cup black beans, drained and rinsed
1/4 cup chopped green onions

● DIRECTIONS ⏱ PREP TIME | 10 MIN 🔲 COOK TIME | 7 MIN

1 | Preheat the air fryer to 350°F (175°C).
2 | Arrange tortilla chips in a single layer in the air fryer basket.
3 | Sprinkle shredded cheddar and Monterey Jack cheese evenly over the chips.
4 | *For Classic Cheese Nachos:*
Add salsa, sliced black olives, and jalapeños to the cheese-covered chips.
5 | *For BBQ Chicken Nachos:*
Mix shredded chicken with BBQ sauce. Spread the BBQ chicken mixture over the cheese-covered chips. Add sliced red onions on top.
6 | *For Loaded Veggie Nachos:*
Sprinkle diced bell peppers, tomatoes, corn kernels, black beans, and chopped green onions over the cheese-covered chips.
7 | Cook in the air fryer for 5-7 minutes until the cheese melts and becomes bubbly.
8 | Carefully remove the nachos from the air fryer and transfer to a serving platter.

LOADED **POTATO SKINS**

● INGREDIENTS 📋 YIELDS | 4 SERVES

6 medium russet potatoes
2 tablespoons olive oil
Salt and pepper to taste
1 cup shredded cheddar cheese

1/2 cup cooked bacon, crumbled
1/2 cup sour cream
2 green onions, sliced
Cooking spray

● DIRECTIONS ⏱ PREP TIME | 15 MIN 🔲 COOK TIME | 14 MIN

1 | Preheat the air fryer to 375°F (190°C). **2 |** Wash and cut the potatoes in half lengthwise. **3 |** Scoop out most of the flesh from each half, leaving about 1/4 inch of the potato in the skin. **4 |** Brush the potato skins with olive oil and season with salt and pepper. **5 |** Place the potato skins in the air fryer basket, skin side down, and cook for 10 minutes until they begin to crisp. **6 |** Sprinkle shredded cheddar cheese evenly into each potato skin. Cook for another 3-4 minutes, until the cheese melts and becomes bubbly. **7 |** Top each potato skin with crumbled bacon, a dollop of sour cream, and sliced green onions. Serve hot.

VARIETY TARTLETS

● **INGREDIENTS** 🍪 **YIELDS | 24 TARTLETS (4 OF EACH TYPE)**

Base Tartlets:
24 mini tartlet shells (store-bought or homemade)

Tomato and Mozzarella Tartlets:
1/2 cup cherry tomatoes, halved
1/2 cup shredded mozzarella cheese
1/4 cup fresh basil leaves, chopped

Bacon and Cheddar Tartlets:
1/2 cup cooked bacon, crumbled
1/2 cup shredded cheddar cheese
1/4 cup green onions, sliced

Apple and Cinnamon Tartlets:
1/2 cup apple, finely diced
1/4 teaspoon ground cinnamon
1 tablespoon brown sugar
1 tablespoon butter, melted

Salmon and Cream Cheese Tarts:
1/2 cup smoked salmon, chopped
1/4 cup cream cheese, softened
1 tablespoon fresh dill, chopped

Tuna and Capers Tarts:
1/2 cup canned tuna, drained and flaked
1 tablespoon capers, drained
1/4 cup mayonnaise
1 tablespoon lemon juice

Crab and Cheddar Tarts:
1/2 cup crab meat, chopped
1/2 cup shredded cheddar cheese
1 tablespoon fresh parsley, chopped

Smoked Trout and Chive Tarts:
1/2 cup smoked trout, flaked
1/4 cup cream cheese, softened
1 tablespoon fresh chives, chopped

● **DIRECTIONS** ⏱ PREP TIME | 20 MIN 📟 COOK TIME | 12 MIN

1 | Preheat the air fryer to 350°F (175°C).

2 | Arrange the tartlet shells in a single layer in the air fryer basket.

3 | For Tomato and Mozzarella Tartlets:
Fill 4 tartlet shells with halved cherry tomatoes and top with shredded mozzarella cheese. Sprinkle with chopped fresh basil.

4 | For Bacon and Cheddar Tartlets:
Fill 4 tartlet shells with crumbled bacon and shredded cheddar cheese. Top with sliced green onions.

5 | For Apple and Cinnamon Tartlets:
Mix diced apple with ground cinnamon, brown sugar, and melted butter in a small bowl.
Fill 4 tartlet shells with the apple mixture.

6 | For Salmon and Cream Cheese Tarts:
Fill 4 tartlet shells with chopped smoked salmon and softened cream cheese. Sprinkle with chopped fresh dill.

7 | For Tuna and Capers Tarts:
Mix flaked tuna with capers, mayonnaise, and lemon juice in a small bowl. Fill 4 tartlet shells with the tuna mixture.

8 | For Crab and Cheddar Tarts:
Fill 4 tartlet shells with chopped crab meat and shredded cheddar cheese. Sprinkle with chopped fresh parsley.

9 | For Smoked Trout and Chive Tarts:
Fill 4 tartlet shells with flaked smoked trout and softened cream cheese. Sprinkle with chopped fresh chives. **10 |** Cook the tartlets in the air fryer for 10-12 minutes until heated and the cheese melts and becomes bubbly. **11 |** Remove the tartlets from the air fryer and let them cool slightly before serving.

VARIETY **SPRING ROLLS**

● **INGREDIENTS**  YIELDS | 24 SPRING ROLLS (8 OF EACH TYPE)

Base Spring Rolls:
24 spring roll wrappers
Cooking spray
Chicken and Veggie Spring Rolls:
1 cup cooked chicken breast,
shredded
1 cup mixed vegetables (carrots,
cabbage, bell pepper), thinly sliced
2 tablespoons soy sauce
1 teaspoon sesame oil

Shrimp and Avocado Spring Rolls:
1 cup cooked shrimp, chopped
1 avocado, diced
1/4 cup fresh cilantro, chopped
1 lime, juiced
Pork and Apple Spring Rolls:
1 cup cooked pork, shredded
1 apple, finely diced
1/4 cup green onions, sliced
1 tablespoon hoisin sauce

● **DIRECTIONS** PREP TIME | 30 MIN COOK TIME | 12 MIN

1 | For Chicken and Veggie Spring Rolls:
Combine shredded chicken, mixed vegetables, soy sauce, and sesame oil in a bowl. Mix well.
Place 2 tablespoons of the mixture onto a spring roll wrapper. Roll tightly, folding in the sides as you go. Repeat for 8 rolls.

2 | For Shrimp and Avocado Spring Rolls:
Combine chopped shrimp, diced avocado, cilantro, and lime juice in a bowl. Mix well.
Place 2 tablespoons of the mixture onto a spring roll wrapper. Roll tightly, folding in the sides as you go. Repeat for 8 rolls.

3 | For Pork and Apple Spring Rolls:
Combine shredded pork, diced apple, green onions, and hoisin sauce in a bowl. Mix well. Place 2 tablespoons of the mixture onto a spring roll wrapper. Roll tightly, folding in the sides as you go. Repeat for 8 rolls.

4 | Preheat the air fryer to 375°F (190°C).

5 | Lightly spray the air fryer basket with cooking spray. Arrange the spring rolls in a single layer in the basket, ensuring they do not touch.

6 | Lightly spray the spring rolls with cooking spray.

7 | Cook in the air fryer for 10-12 minutes, turning halfway through, until the spring rolls are golden brown and crispy.

8 | Remove from the air fryer and let cool slightly before serving.

VARIETY QUESADILLAS

● **INGREDIENTS** 📚 YIELDS | 6 QUESADILLAS (2 OF EACH TYPE)

6 large flour tortillas
2 cups shredded cheese (cheddar
or a cheese blend)
Cooking spray
For Classic Cheese Quesadilla:
1 cup shredded cheese (cheddar or
a cheese blend)

For Chicken and Spinach Quesadilla:
1 cup cooked chicken, shredded
1 cup fresh spinach, chopped
1 cup shredded cheese (cheddar or a
cheese blend)
For BBQ Chicken Quesadilla:
1 cup cooked chicken, shredded
1/4 cup BBQ sauce
1 cup shredded cheese (cheddar or a
cheese blend)

● **DIRECTIONS** ⏱ PREP TIME | 15 MIN 🍳 COOK TIME | 10 MIN

1 | Preheat the air fryer to 375°F (190°C). **2 |** Lightly spray the air fryer basket with cooking spray. Place a tortilla on a flat surface.
3 | *Classic Cheese Quesadilla:*
Sprinkle 1/2 cup of shredded cheese evenly over one-half of a tortilla. Fold the tortilla in half to cover the cheese.
4 | *Chicken and Spinach Quesadilla:*
Mix shredded chicken and chopped spinach in a bowl. Sprinkle 1/2 cup of the mixture and 1/2 cup of shredded cheese evenly over half of a tortilla. Fold the tortilla in half to cover the filling.
5 | *BBQ Chicken Quesadilla:*
Mix shredded chicken with BBQ sauce in a bowl. Sprinkle 1/2 cup of the mixture and 1/2 cup of shredded cheese evenly over half of a tortilla. Fold the tortilla in half to cover the filling.
6 | Place the folded quesadillas in the air fryer basket, ensuring they do not overlap. Cook for 8-10 minutes, flipping halfway through, until the tortillas crisp up and the cheese melts.

BACON-WRAPPED SAUSAGE BITES

● **INGREDIENTS** 📚 YIELDS | 4 SERVES

8 sausage links (breakfast sausages or
your favorite type)
8 slices of bacon

1/4 cup maple syrup (optional for glazing)
Toothpicks
Cooking spray

● **DIRECTIONS** ⏱ PREP TIME | 10 MIN 🍳 COOK TIME | 15 MIN

1 | Cut the bacon slices in half. Wrap each sausage link with a half slice of bacon, securing it with a toothpick.
2 | If desired, brush each bacon-wrapped sausage with maple syrup for added sweetness.
3 | Preheat the air fryer to 375°F (190°C) for about 5 minutes.
4 | Lightly spray the air fryer basket with cooking spray. Arrange the bacon-wrapped sausages in a single layer in the basket, ensuring they do not overlap.
5 | Cook at 375°F (190°C) for 12-15 minutes, turning halfway through, until the bacon crisps and the sausages are cooked through.
6 | Remove the sausage bites from the air fryer and let them cool slightly before serving.

VARIETY STUFFED JALAPEÑOS

● INGREDIENTS YIELDS | 36 STUFFED JALAPEÑOS (12 OF EACH TYPE)

18 large jalapeños, halved and seeded (36 halves)
Cooking spray
For Bacon-Wrapped Stuffed Jalapeños:
12 slices of bacon, cut in half
1 cup cream cheese, softened
1/2 cup shredded cheddar cheese
For Cheddar and Sausage Stuffed Jalapeños:
1 cup cooked sausage, crumbled
1 cup shredded cheddar cheese

For Buffalo Chicken Stuffed Jalapeños:
1 cup cooked chicken, shredded
1/4 cup Buffalo sauce
1/2 cup cream cheese, softened
1/4 cup blue cheese crumbles

● DIRECTIONS ⏱ PREP TIME | 20 MIN 🍳 COOK TIME | 12 MIN

1 | Preheat the air fryer to 375°F (190°C).
2 | *Bacon-Wrapped Stuffed Jalapeños:*
Mix cream cheese and shredded cheddar cheese in a bowl until well combined. Fill 12 jalapeño halves with the cheese mixture. Wrap each stuffed jalapeño half with a half slice of bacon, securing with a toothpick if needed.
3 | *Cheddar and Sausage Stuffed Jalapeños:*
In a bowl, mix crumbled cooked sausage and shredded cheddar cheese. Fill 12 jalapeño halves with the sausage and cheese mixture.
4 | *Buffalo Chicken Stuffed Jalapeños:*
Mix shredded chicken, Buffalo sauce, and cream cheese in a bowl until well combined.
Fill 12 jalapeño halves with the Buffalo chicken mixture. Sprinkle blue cheese crumbles on top.
5 | Lightly spray the air fryer basket with cooking spray. Arrange the stuffed jalapeños in a single layer in the basket, ensuring they do not overlap. **6 |** Cook for 10-12 minutes or until the jalapeños are tender and the fillings are hot and bubbly.

MAC AND **CHEESE BALLS**

● **INGREDIENTS** 🍽 YIELDS | 4 SERVES

2 cups cooked macaroni
2 cups shredded cheddar cheese
1/2 cup grated Parmesan cheese
1/2 cup all-purpose flour
2 large eggs

1 cup bread crumbs (panko or regular)
1/2 teaspoon garlic powder (optional)
1/2 teaspoon onion powder (optional)
Salt and pepper to taste
Cooking spray or oil for air frying

● **DIRECTIONS** ⏱ PREP TIME | 20 MIN 📟 COOK TIME | 10 MIN

1 | Combine the cooked macaroni, shredded cheddar cheese, grated Parmesan cheese, garlic powder, onion powder, salt, and pepper in a large bowl. Mix well until all ingredients are evenly combined. Using your hands, form the mac and cheese mixture into small balls, about 1-2 inches in diameter. Place them on a baking sheet lined with parchment paper. **2 |** Set up a breading station with three bowls: one with flour, one with beaten eggs, and one with bread crumbs. Roll each mac and cheese ball in the flour, shaking off excess. Dip the ball into the beaten eggs, letting any excess drip off. Roll the ball in the bread crumbs, pressing gently to adhere. Place the coated balls back on the baking sheet. **3 |** Preheat the air fryer to 375°F (190°C). **4 |** Lightly spray or brush the mac and cheese balls with oil. Place the balls in the air fryer basket in a single layer, ensuring they are not touching. Air fry for 8-10 minutes, turning halfway through, until they are golden brown and crispy. **5 |** Allow the mac and cheese balls to cool for a few minutes before serving. Serve with your favorite dipping sauces, such as marinara, ranch, or cheese sauce.

BUFFALO **CHICKEN WONTONS**

● **INGREDIENTS** 🍽 YIELDS | 4 SERVES

1 cup cooked chicken, shredded
1/4 cup buffalo sauce
1/4 cup cream cheese, softened
1/2 cup shredded cheddar cheese

2 tablespoons chopped green onions
24 wonton wrappers
1 egg, beaten (for sealing)
Cooking spray or oil for air frying

● **DIRECTIONS** ⏱ PREP TIME | 20 MIN 📟 COOK TIME | 10 MIN

1 | Mix the shredded chicken, buffalo sauce, cream cheese, cheddar cheese, and chopped green onions in a medium bowl until well combined.
2 | Lay a wonton wrapper on a clean surface. Place about 1 tablespoon of the buffalo chicken filling in the center of the wrapper. Brush the edges of the wrapper with the beaten egg. Fold the wrapper in half diagonally to form a triangle, pressing the edges to seal. Make sure there are no air bubbles. Optionally, bring the two opposite corners of the triangle together and press to seal, creating a more compact shape.
3 | Preheat the air fryer to 375°F (190°C).
4 | Lightly spray or brush the wontons with oil. Place the wontons in a single layer in the air fryer basket, ensuring they are not touching. Air fry for 6-8 minutes, turning halfway through, until the wontons are golden brown and crispy.
5 | Allow the wontons to cool for a few minutes before serving. Serve with your favorite dipping sauce, ranch, or blue cheese dressing.

VEGAN STUFFED MUSHROOMS

● INGREDIENTS  YIELDS | 4 SERVES

16 large button mushrooms, stems removed and finely chopped
2 tablespoons olive oil
1 small onion, finely diced
2 cloves garlic, minced
1/2 cup breadcrumbs (use gluten-free if needed)

1/4 cup nutritional yeast
1/4 cup chopped fresh parsley
1 tablespoon soy sauce (or tamari for gluten-free)
1 teaspoon dried thyme
Salt and pepper to taste
Cooking spray

● DIRECTIONS ⏱ PREP TIME | 15 MIN 🍳 COOK TIME | 10 MIN

1 | In a skillet over medium heat, heat olive oil and sauté the diced onion and minced garlic until softened, about 3-4 minutes. Add the chopped mushroom stems and cook until they release moisture and become tender, about 5 minutes. **2 |** Remove the skillet from heat and stir in the breadcrumbs, nutritional yeast, chopped parsley, soy sauce, dried thyme, salt, and pepper. Mix well until the stuffing is well combined. **3 |** Preheat the air fryer to 375°F (190°C). **4 |** Lightly spray the air fryer basket with cooking spray. Stuff each mushroom cap with the prepared filling, pressing gently to compact the mixture. **5 |** Place the stuffed mushrooms in the air fryer basket in a single layer. Cook at 375°F (190°C) for 10 minutes or until the mushrooms are tender and the tops are golden brown. **6 |** Serve hot, garnished with additional chopped parsley if desired.

SPICY CHICKPEA PATTIES

● INGREDIENTS  YIELDS | 4 SERVES

1 can (15 oz) chickpeas, drained and rinsed
1 small onion, finely diced
2 cloves garlic, minced
1/4 cup fresh parsley, chopped
1/4 cup breadcrumbs (use gluten-free if needed)
2 tablespoons chickpea flour
1 tablespoon olive oil

1 teaspoon ground cumin
1 teaspoon ground coriander
1/2 teaspoon paprika
1/2 teaspoon chili powder
1/4 teaspoon cayenne pepper (adjust to taste)
Salt and pepper to taste
Cooking spray

● DIRECTIONS ⏱ PREP TIME | 15 MIN 🍳 COOK TIME | 12 MIN

1 | In a food processor, pulse the chickpeas until they are coarsely mashed. Transfer to a large bowl. **2 |** Add the diced onion, minced garlic, chopped parsley, breadcrumbs, chickpea flour, olive oil, ground cumin, ground coriander, paprika, chili powder, cayenne pepper, salt, and pepper to the bowl. Mix well until all ingredients are combined.
3 | Form the mixture into small patties about 2 inches in diameter. **4 |** Preheat the air fryer to 375°F (190°C). **5 |** Lightly spray the air fryer basket with cooking spray. Place the patties in the basket in a single layer, ensuring they do not touch. **6 |** Cook at 375°F (190°C) for 10-12 minutes, flipping halfway through, until the patties are golden brown and crispy. **7 |** Serve hot with your favorite dipping sauce or in a pita with vegetables.
Note: If the mixture is too wet to form patties, add more breadcrumbs until it reaches the desired consistency.

RED PEPPER **HUMMUS**

 **INGREDIENTS** YIELDS | 4 SERVES

For the Roasted Red Pepper Hummus:
1 can (15 oz) chickpeas, drained and rinsed
1 large roasted red pepper, chopped (you can use store-bought or roast your own)
1/4 cup tahini
2 tablespoons lemon juice
2 tablespoons olive oil
2 cloves garlic, minced

1/2 teaspoon ground cumin
Salt and pepper to taste
2-3 tablespoons water (adjust for desired consistency)
For the Pita Chips:
4 whole wheat pita bread rounds
2 tablespoons olive oil
1 teaspoon garlic powder
1 teaspoon paprika
Salt to taste
Cooking spray

 **DIRECTIONS**  PREP TIME | 1 MIN COOK TIME | 1 MIN

1 | Combine chickpeas, roasted red pepper, tahini, lemon juice, olive oil, minced garlic, ground cumin, salt, and pepper in a food processor. Process until smooth, adding water and one tablespoon until you reach the desired consistency. Taste and adjust seasoning as needed. Transfer the hummus to a serving bowl. **2 |** Preheat the air fryer to 350°F (175°C). Cut each pita bread round into 8 triangles. Mix the olive oil, garlic powder, paprika, and salt in a small bowl. Brush the pita triangles with the seasoned oil mixture. Lightly spray the air fryer basket with cooking spray. Place the pita triangles in the basket in a single layer, working in batches if necessary. Cook at 350°F (175°C) for 8-10 minutes, flipping halfway through, until the pita chips are golden brown and crispy.

3 | Serve the roasted red pepper hummus with the warm pita chips. Enjoy as a delicious appetizer or snack!

Note: Roast your red peppers by placing them under a broiler until the skin chars, then peel off the skin and remove the seeds.

CRISPY **AVOCADO FRIES**

● **INGREDIENTS** 🍽 YIELDS | 4 SERVES

2 ripe avocados
1/2 cup all-purpose flour
2 large eggs, beaten
1 cup panko breadcrumbs
1/2 teaspoon garlic powder

1/2 teaspoon paprika
1/2 teaspoon salt
1/4 teaspoon black pepper
Cooking spray

● **DIRECTIONS** ⏱ PREP TIME | 10 MIN 📟 COOK TIME | 10 MIN

1 | Preheat the air fryer to 400°F (200°C). **2 |** Cut the avocados, remove the pit, and slice each half into 4-6 wedges. **3 |** Set up a breading station with three bowls: one with flour, one with beaten eggs, and one with a mixture of panko breadcrumbs, garlic powder, paprika, salt, and black pepper. **4 |** Dredge each avocado wedge in flour, shaking off any excess. Dip into the beaten eggs, then coat with the panko breadcrumb mixture, pressing gently to adhere. **5 |** Lightly spray the air fryer basket with cooking spray. Place the breaded avocado wedges in a single layer in the basket, working in batches if necessary. **6 |** Cook at 400°F (200°C) for 10 minutes, flipping halfway through, until the avocado fries are golden brown and crispy. **7 |** Serve immediately with your favorite dipping sauce.

SWEET AND SPICY **MEATBALLS**

● **INGREDIENTS** 🍽 YIELDS | 4 SERVES

1 pound ground beef or pork
1/2 cup breadcrumbs
1/4 cup milk
1 large egg
1/4 cup finely chopped onion
2 cloves garlic, minced
1/4 teaspoon salt
tablespoon sriracha or hot sauce

1/4 teaspoon black pepper
1/2 teaspoon paprika
1/4 teaspoon cayenne pepper
(optional for extra spice)
1/2 cup sweet chili sauce
2 tablespoons soy sauce
2 tablespoons honey
Cooking spray

● **DIRECTIONS** ⏱ PREP TIME | 15 MIN 📟 COOK TIME | 15 MIN

1 | Combine the ground beef or pork, breadcrumbs, milk, egg, chopped onion, minced garlic, salt, black pepper, paprika, and cayenne pepper in a large bowl. Mix until well combined. **2 |** Form the mixture into 1-inch meatballs. **3 |** Preheat the air fryer to 375°F (190°C). **4 |** Lightly spray the air fryer basket with cooking spray. Place the meatballs in a single layer in the basket, working in batches if necessary. **5 |** Cook the meatballs at 375°F (190°C) for 12-15 minutes, shaking the basket halfway through, until browned and cooked through. **6 |** While the meatballs are cooking, mix the sweet chili sauce, soy sauce, honey, and sriracha or hot sauce in a small bowl. **7 |** Transfer the cooked meatballs to a large bowl. Pour the sauce over the meatballs and toss to coat them evenly. **8 |** Serve immediately with toothpicks or over rice for a complete meal.

MINI PHILLY **CHEESESTEAK BITES**

● **INGREDIENTS** 🍽 **YIELDS** | 4 SERVES

1/2 pound thinly sliced beef steak
(such as ribeye)
1/2 green bell pepper, finely chopped
1/2 onion, finely chopped
1/2 cup shredded provolone cheese
1 tablespoon olive oil

1/2 teaspoon salt
1/4 teaspoon black pepper
1/4 teaspoon garlic powder
1/4 teaspoon onion powder
12 mini phyllo pastry cups
Cooking spray

● **DIRECTIONS** ⏱ PREP TIME | 15 MIN 🍳 COOK TIME | 12 MIN

1 | Warm the olive oil in a skillet over medium heat. Add the chopped onion and green bell pepper, and cook until softened about 5 minutes.
2 | Add the thinly sliced beef steak to the skillet—season with salt, black pepper, garlic powder, and onion powder. Cook until the beef is no longer pink, about 3-4 minutes.
3 | Stir in the shredded provolone cheese until melted and combined with the beef mixture. Remove from heat. **4 |** Preheat the air fryer to 375°F (190°C). **5 |** Lightly spray the air fryer basket with cooking spray. Place the mini phyllo pastry cups in the basket in a single layer. **6 |** Fill each phyllo cup with the cheesesteak mixture. **7 |** Cook in the air fryer at 375°F (190°C) for 10-12 minutes until the phyllo cups are golden brown and crispy. **8 |** Remove from the air fryer and let cool slightly before serving.

MEXICAN **STREET CORN BITES**

● **INGREDIENTS** 🍽 **YIELDS** | 4 SERVES

2 cups corn kernels (fresh, frozen, or
canned)
1/2 cup crumbled cotija cheese (or
feta cheese)
1/4 cup mayonnaise
1/4 cup sour cream
1/2 teaspoon chili powder

1/4 teaspoon smoked paprika
1 clove garlic, minced
1 tablespoon fresh lime juice
2 tablespoons chopped fresh cilantro
Salt and pepper to taste
Cooking spray
Lime wedges for serving

● **DIRECTIONS** ⏱ PREP TIME | 10 MIN 🍳 COOK TIME | 10 MIN

1 | Mix the corn kernels, mayonnaise, sour cream, chili powder, smoked paprika, minced garlic, lime juice, salt, and pepper in a large bowl until well combined. **2 |** Preheat the air fryer to 375°F (190°C). **3 |** Lightly spray the air fryer basket with cooking spray. Spoon the corn mixture into tiny, bite-sized heaps in the basket, leaving some space between each heap. **4 |** Cook in the air fryer at 375°F (190°C) for 8-10 minutes, until the corn lightly chars and the mixture heats through. **5 |** Remove the corn bites from the air fryer and place them on a serving plate. **6 |** Sprinkle the crumbled cotija cheese and chopped cilantro over the corn bites. **7 |** Serve immediately with lime wedges on the side.

THAI CHICKEN **SATAY SKEWERS**

● **INGREDIENTS** 🍽 **YIELDS** | 4 SERVES

1 lb (450 g) chicken breast, cut into thin strips
1/2 cup coconut milk
2 tablespoons soy sauce
2 tablespoons brown sugar
1 tablespoon curry powder
1 teaspoon ground coriander
1 teaspoon ground cumin
1 teaspoon turmeric powder
2 cloves garlic, minced
1 tablespoon fresh lime juice

Skewers (if using wooden skewers, soak them in water for 30 minutes)
For the Peanut Sauce:
1/2 cup peanut butter
1/2 cup coconut milk
1 tablespoon soy sauce
1 tablespoon brown sugar
1 tablespoon lime juice
1 teaspoon chili paste or sriracha (adjust to taste)
1 clove garlic, minced

● **DIRECTIONS** ⏱ PREP TIME | 15 MIN 📠 COOK TIME | 15 MIN

1 | Mix coconut milk, soy sauce, brown sugar, curry powder, ground coriander, ground cumin, turmeric powder, minced garlic, and lime juice in a large bowl. **2 |** Add the chicken strips to the marinade, ensuring they are well coated. Cover and marinate in the refrigerator for at least 30 minutes or 2 hours for the best flavor. **3 |** Preheat the air fryer to 375°F (190°C). **4 |** Thread the marinated chicken strips onto the skewers.
5 | Lightly spray the air fryer basket with cooking spray. Place the skewers in the basket in a single layer. **6 |** Cook at 375°F (190°C) for 12-15 minutes, turning halfway through, until the chicken is cooked through and slightly charred on the edges. **7 |** While the chicken is cooking, prepare the peanut sauce. Combine peanut butter, coconut milk, soy sauce, brown sugar, lime juice, chili paste, and minced garlic in a small saucepan over medium heat. Stir until smooth and heated through. Remove from heat. **8 |** For dipping, serve the Thai Chicken Satay Skewers hot with the peanut sauce on the side.

BAKED **BRIE BITES**

● **INGREDIENTS** 🍽 YIELDS | 4 SERVES

1 sheet puff pastry, thawed
8 oz Brie cheese, cut into 24 small cubes
1/4 cup honey

1/4 cup chopped pecans or walnuts
1/4 cup cranberry sauce or jam (optional)
Cooking spray

● **DIRECTIONS** ⏱ PREP TIME | 10 MIN 📠 COOK TIME | 10 MIN

1 | Roll out the puff pastry sheet on a lightly floured surface to smooth any creases.
2 | Cut the puff pastry into 24 equal squares. **3 |** Place a cube of Brie cheese in the center of each puff pastry square. **4 |** Drizzle a small amount of honey over each piece of cheese. **5 |** Sprinkle chopped pecans or walnuts on top of the honey. If desired, add a small dollop of cranberry sauce or jam. **6 |** Bring the corners of each puff pastry square together to form a small bundle, pinching the edges to seal. **7 |** Preheat the air fryer to 375°F (190°C) for about 5 minutes. **8 |** Lightly spray the air fryer basket with cooking spray. Place the Brie bites in the basket, ensuring they do not touch. **9 |** Cook in the air fryer for 8-10 minutes or until the pastry is golden brown and puffed.
10 | Remove from the air fryer and let cool slightly before serving.

CRISPY MOZZARELLA STICKS

● **INGREDIENTS** 🍽 YIELDS | 4 SERVES

12 mozzarella cheese sticks
1 cup all-purpose flour
2 large eggs, beaten
1 cup seasoned breadcrumbs
1/2 teaspoon garlic powder

1/2 teaspoon onion powder
1/2 teaspoon Italian seasoning
Cooking spray
Marinara sauce for dipping

● **DIRECTIONS** ⏱ PREP TIME | 15 MIN 🍳 COOK TIME | 10 MIN

1 | Prepare three separate bowls: one with flour, one with beaten eggs, and one with seasoned breadcrumbs mixed with garlic powder, onion powder, and Italian seasoning.
2 | Dip each mozzarella stick into the flour, coating evenly. Then, dip it into the beaten eggs, and finally, coat it with the breadcrumb mixture, pressing gently to adhere the breadcrumbs.
3 | Repeat the coating process for each mozzarella stick to ensure a thick, crispy layer.
4 | Place the coated mozzarella sticks on a baking sheet and freeze for at least 1 hour to prevent the cheese from melting during cooking.
5 | Preheat the air fryer to 400°F (200°C).
6 | Lightly spray the air fryer basket with cooking spray. Place the frozen mozzarella sticks in a single layer in the basket, ensuring they do not touch.
7 | Cook in the air fryer for 8-10 minutes, or until the mozzarella sticks are golden brown and crispy, flipping them halfway through the cooking time.
8 | Serve immediately with marinara sauce for dipping.

SOUTHWEST EGG ROLLS

● **INGREDIENTS** 🍽 YIELDS | 4 SERVES

1 cup cooked chicken, shredded
1/2 cup black beans, drained and rinsed
1/2 cup corn kernels
1/2 cup diced red bell pepper
1/4 cup diced green onions
1/4 cup chopped fresh cilantro
1 cup shredded Monterey Jack cheese

1 teaspoon ground cumin
1 teaspoon chili powder
1/2 teaspoon garlic powder
1/2 teaspoon salt
8 egg roll wrappers
Cooking spray
Salsa and sour cream for dipping

● **DIRECTIONS** ⏱ PREP TIME | 20 MIN 🍳 COOK TIME | 12 MIN

1 | Combine the shredded chicken, black beans, corn, red bell pepper, green onions, cilantro, shredded Monterey Jack cheese, ground cumin, chili powder, garlic powder, and salt in a large bowl. Mix until well combined. **2 |** Lay an egg roll wrapper on a clean surface with one corner pointing towards you. Place 2-3 tablespoons of the chicken mixture in the center of the wrapper.
3 | Fold the bottom corner over the filling, then fold in the sides and roll up tightly. Use a bit of water to seal the edges of the wrapper. Repeat with the remaining wrappers and filling.
4 | Preheat the air fryer to 375°F (190°C). **5 |** Lightly spray the air fryer basket with cooking spray. Place the egg rolls in a single layer in the basket, ensuring they do not touch. **6 |** Cook in the air fryer for 10-12 minutes or until the egg rolls are golden brown and crispy, turning them halfway through the cooking time. **7 |** Serve immediately with salsa and sour cream for dipping.

CHAPTER 8

SWEET & SAVORY AIR FRYER BAKES & GOODIES

DECADENT **FUDGE BROWNIES**

● **INGREDIENTS** 📚 **YIELDS** | 12 BROWNIES

1/2 cup unsalted butter, melted
1 cup granulated sugar
2 large eggs
1 teaspoon vanilla extract
1/3 cup cocoa powder

1/2 cup all-purpose flour
1/4 teaspoon salt
1/4 teaspoon baking powder
1 cup semi-sweet chocolate chips

● **DIRECTIONS** ⏱ PREP TIME | 15 MIN ⬛ COOK TIME | 25 MIN

1 | Mix the melted butter and granulated sugar in a large bowl until smooth. Add the eggs and vanilla extract, beating until well combined. **2 |** Sift in the cocoa powder, flour, salt, and baking powder. Mix until just combined, then fold in the semi-sweet chocolate chips. **3 |** Preheat the air fryer to 320°F (160°C) for about 3 minutes. Line a small, air fryer-safe baking pan with parchment paper, leaving some overhang for easy removal.
4 | Pour the brownie batter into the prepared pan, spreading it evenly. **5 |** Place the pan in the air fryer basket and cook for 20-25 minutes, or until a toothpick inserted into the center comes out with a few moist crumbs. **6 |** Remove the brownies from the air fryer and let them cool in the pan for 10 minutes. Using the parchment paper overhang, lift the brownies out of the pan and transfer them to a wire rack to cool completely.

IRRESISTIBLE **PUMPKIN SPICE DELIGHT PIE**

● **INGREDIENTS** 📚 **YIELDS** | 6-8 SLICES

1 pre-made pie crust
1 cup canned pumpkin puree
1/2 cup evaporated milk
1/2 cup granulated sugar
1 large egg

1 teaspoon ground cinnamon
1/2 teaspoon ground ginger
1/4 teaspoon ground cloves
1/4 teaspoon salt

● **DIRECTIONS** ⏱ PREP TIME | 15 MIN ⬛ COOK TIME | 25 MIN

1 | Preheat the air fryer to 320°F (160°C). **2 |** Roll out the pre-made pie crust and place it in a small, air fryer-safe dish. **3 |** Whisk together the pumpkin puree, evaporated milk, granulated sugar, egg, cinnamon, ginger, cloves, and salt in a large bowl until smooth. **4 |** Pour the pumpkin mixture into the pie crust. **5 |** Place the pie dish in the air fryer basket and cook for 20-25 minutes until the filling sets and the crust turns golden brown. **6 |** Remove the pie from the air fryer and let it cool before serving.

NEW YORK **INDULGENCE CHEESECAKE**

● INGREDIENTS  YIELDS | 1 CHEESECAKE

For the crust:
1 1/2 cups graham cracker crumbs
1/4 cup granulated sugar
1/2 cup unsalted butter, melted
For the filling:
4 (8 oz) packages of cream cheese, softened

1 1/4 cups granulated sugar
1 teaspoon vanilla extract
4 large eggs
1 cup sour cream
1/2 cup heavy cream

● DIRECTIONS ⏱ PREP TIME | 20 MIN 🔲 COOK TIME | 50 MIN

1 | Mix the graham cracker crumbs, sugar, and melted butter in a medium bowl until well combined. Press the mixture firmly into the bottom of a greased 7-inch springform pan. Place the pan in the refrigerator to chill while preparing the filling. **2 |** In a large bowl, beat the softened cream cheese until smooth and creamy. Gradually add the sugar and continue to beat until well combined. Mix in the vanilla extract. **3 |** Add the eggs, one at a time, beating well after each addition. Add the sour and heavy cream, and mix until the batter is smooth and well combined. **4 |** Pour the filling over the prepared crust in the springform pan. Smooth the top with a spatula. **5 |** Preheat the air fryer to 325°F (165°C). **6 |** Preheat the air fryer and place the springform pan inside. Bake for 45-50 minutes until the edges are set and the center is slightly jiggly. Turn off the air fryer and let the cheesecake sit for 30 minutes. **7 |** Remove the cheesecake from the air fryer and let it cool at room temperature. Once cooled, refrigerate for at least 4 hours or overnight to set.

PEANUT BUTTER **SWIRL BROWNIES**

● INGREDIENTS  YIELDS | 12 BROWNIES

1/2 cup unsalted butter, melted
1 cup granulated sugar
2 large eggs
1 teaspoon vanilla extract
1/3 cup cocoa powder
1/2 cup all-purpose flour

1/4 teaspoon salt
1/4 teaspoon baking powder
1/2 cup creamy peanut butter, slightly melted
1/2 cup semi-sweet chocolate chips

● DIRECTIONS ⏱ PREP TIME | 15 MIN 🔲 COOK TIME | 25 MIN

1 | Mix the melted butter and granulated sugar in a large bowl until smooth. Add the eggs and vanilla extract, beating until well combined. **2 |** Sift in the cocoa powder, flour, salt, and baking powder. Mix until just combined, then fold in the semi-sweet chocolate chips. **3 |** Preheat the air fryer to 320°F (160°C) for about 3 minutes. Line a small, air fryer-safe baking pan with parchment paper, leaving some overhang for easy removal. **4 |** Pour the brownie batter into the prepared pan, spreading it evenly. Drizzle the melted peanut butter over the brownie batter. Use a knife or toothpick to swirl the peanut butter into the batter. **5 |** Place the pan in the air fryer basket and cook for 20-25 minutes, or until a toothpick inserted into the center comes out with a few moist crumbs. **6 |** Remove the brownies from the air fryer and let them cool in the pan for 10 minutes. Using the parchment paper overhang, lift the brownies out of the pan and transfer them to a wire rack to cool completely.

S'MORES **BROWNIE BARS**

INGREDIENTS  YIELDS | 12 BARS

1/2 cup unsalted butter, melted
1 cup granulated sugar
2 large eggs
1 teaspoon vanilla extract
1/3 cup cocoa powder
1/2 cup all-purpose flour

1/4 teaspoon salt
1/4 teaspoon baking powder
1 cup semi-sweet chocolate chips
1 cup graham cracker crumbs
1 cup mini marshmallows

DIRECTIONS PREP TIME | 15 MIN COOK TIME | 25 MIN

1 | Mix the melted butter and granulated sugar in a large bowl until smooth. Add the eggs and vanilla extract, beating until well combined. **2 |** Sift in the cocoa powder, flour, salt, and baking powder. Mix until just combined, then fold in the semi-sweet chocolate chips. **3 |** Preheat the air fryer to 320°F (160°C) for about 3 minutes. **4 |** Line a small, air fryer-safe baking pan with parchment paper, leaving some overhang for easy removal. **5 |** Pour half of the brownie batter into the prepared pan, spreading it evenly. Sprinkle a layer of graham cracker crumbs and mini marshmallows over the batter. Pour the remaining brownie batter and spread evenly to cover the marshmallows and graham cracker crumbs. **6 |** Place the pan in the air fryer basket and cook for 20-25 minutes, or until a toothpick inserted into the center comes out with a few moist crumbs. **7 |** Remove the brownies from the air fryer and let them cool in the pan for 10 minutes. Using the parchment paper overhang, lift the brownies out of the pan and transfer them to a wire rack to cool completely.

CARAMEL APPLE **CRUMBLE PIE**

INGREDIENTS  YIELDS | 6 SERVES

For the Crust:
1 store-bought pie crust or homemade
crust of your choice
For the Filling:
6 cups thinly sliced apples (Granny
Smith or Honeycrisp recommended)
1/2 cup granulated sugar
1/4 cup packed brown sugar
2 tablespoons all-purpose flour
1 teaspoon ground cinnamon
1/4 teaspoon ground nutmeg

1/4 teaspoon salt
1 teaspoon vanilla extract
1/2 cup caramel sauce (store-bought or
homemade)
For the Crumble Topping:
1/2 cup all-purpose flour
1/2 cup rolled oats
1/3 cup packed brown sugar
1/2 teaspoon ground cinnamon
1/4 cup unsalted butter, cold and cubed

DIRECTIONS PREP TIME | 20 MIN COOK TIME | 30 MIN

1 | Place the pie crust into a dish, crimping the edges as desired. Combine the sliced apples, granulated sugar, brown sugar, flour, cinnamon, nutmeg, salt, and vanilla extract in a large bowl. Toss until the apples are well coated. **2 |** Preheat the air fryer to 350°F (175°C). Pour the apple mixture into the prepared pie crust and drizzle the caramel sauce over the top. **3 |** Mix the flour, oats, brown sugar, and cinnamon in a separate bowl for the crumble topping. Cut in the cold, cubed butter until the mixture resembles coarse crumbs. Sprinkle the crumble topping evenly over the caramel-covered apples. **4 |** Place the pie dish in the air fryer basket. Air fry for 25-30 minutes or until the topping is golden brown and the filling is bubbly. **5 |** Allow the pie to cool slightly on a wire rack before serving.

HEAVENLY BANANA NUT DELIGHT MUFFINS

● INGREDIENTS 🍽️ YIELDS | 12 MUFFINS

3 ripe bananas, mashed
1/2 cup unsalted butter, melted
1/2 cup granulated sugar
1/4 cup brown sugar
2 large eggs
1 teaspoon vanilla extract
1 1/2 cups all-purpose flour

1 1/2 teaspoons baking powder
1/4 teaspoon baking soda
1/2 teaspoon salt
1/2 cup chopped walnuts
1/2 teaspoon ground cinnamon
(optional)

● DIRECTIONS ⏱️ PREP TIME | 15 MIN 🍳 COOK TIME | 18 MIN

1 | Line your muffin tin with paper liners or lightly grease them. Preheat your air fryer to 350°F (175°C). **2 |** Combine the mashed bananas and melted butter in a large mixing bowl until well blended. Add granulated and brown sugar to the banana mixture, stirring until smooth. Beat in the eggs, one at a time, followed by the vanilla extract. **3 |** Whisk together the flour, baking powder, baking soda, and salt in a separate bowl. Gradually add the dry ingredients to the banana mixture, mixing until combined. Be careful not to overmix. Fold in the chopped walnuts and ground cinnamon (if using). **4 |** Spoon the batter evenly into the prepared muffin tin, filling each cup about 2/3 full. **5 |** Place the muffin tin in the preheated air fryer and bake for 15-18 minutes, or until a toothpick inserted into the center of a muffin comes out clean. Allow the muffins to cool in the tin for a few minutes before transferring them to a wire rack to cool completely.

IRRESISTIBLE CINNAMON ROLL RECIPES

● INGREDIENTS 🍽️ YIELDS | 12 ROLLS

2 3/4 cups all-purpose flour
3 tablespoons granulated sugar
1 teaspoon salt
1 packet active dry yeast (2 1/4 teaspoons)
1/2 cup whole milk

1/4 cup water
1/4 cup unsalted butter, melted
1 large egg
1/4 cup unsalted butter, softened
1/2 cup granulated sugar
2 tablespoons ground cinnamon

● DIRECTIONS ⏱️ PREP TIME | 1 HOUR 30 MIN 🍳 COOK TIME | 15 MIN

1 | Combine 2 1/4 cups of flour, granulated sugar, salt, and yeast in a large bowl. **2 |** Heat the milk and water in a small saucepan until warm (about 110°F/45°C). Add the melted butter to the milk mixture. **3 |** Gradually add the milk mixture to the flour mixture, beating slowly until well combined. Add the egg and beat until smooth. Stir in the remaining flour to form a soft dough. **4 |** Knead the dough on a floured surface for about 5 minutes until smooth and elastic. Place the dough in a greased bowl, cover it, and let it rise in a warm place until doubled in size (about 1 hour). **5 |** Preheat the air fryer to 375°F (190°C). **6 |** Roll out the dough into a 12x8-inch rectangle. Spread the softened butter over the dough. Mix the granulated sugar and cinnamon and sprinkle it evenly over the buttered dough. **7 |** Roll up the dough tightly, starting from the long side. Cut into 12 rolls and place them in a greased air fryer basket. **8 |** Bake for 12-15 minutes or until golden brown. **9 |** Allow the rolls to cool slightly before serving.

STICKY PECAN **BLISS ROLLS**

● INGREDIENTS YIELDS | 12 ROLLS

2 3/4 cups all-purpose flour
3 tablespoons granulated sugar
1 teaspoon salt
1 packet active dry yeast (2 1/4 teaspoons)
1/2 cup whole milk
1/4 cup water
1/4 cup unsalted butter, melted

1 large egg
1/4 cup unsalted butter, softened
1/2 cup granulated sugar
2 tablespoons ground cinnamon
1/2 cup chopped pecans
1/2 cup brown sugar
1/4 cup unsalted butter, melted
2 tablespoons honey

● DIRECTIONS PREP TIME | 1 HOUR 30 MIN COOK TIME | 15 MIN

1 | Follow steps 1-6 from the Heavenly Classic Cinnamon Swirls recipe. **2 |** Preheat the air fryer to 375°F (190°C). **3 |** Roll out the dough into a 12x8-inch rectangle. Spread the softened butter over the dough. Mix the granulated sugar and cinnamon and sprinkle it evenly over the buttered dough. **4 |** Roll up the dough tightly, starting from the long side. Cut into 12 rolls. **5 |** Mix the chopped pecans, brown sugar, melted butter, and honey in a small bowl. Spread this mixture on the bottom of a greased air fryer basket. **6 |** Place the rolls on top of the pecan mixture. **7 |** Bake for 12-15 minutes or until golden brown. **8 |** Allow the rolls to cool slightly before inverting the basket to remove the rolls and the sticky pecan topping.

ULTIMATE BANANA **BLISS BREAD**

● INGREDIENTS YIELDS | 4 LOAF

1 1/2 cups all-purpose flour
1 teaspoon baking soda
1/4 teaspoon salt
1/2 cup unsalted butter, softened
3/4 cup brown sugar
2 large eggs, beaten

1 1/2 cups mashed overripe bananas (about 3-4 bananas)
1 teaspoon vanilla extract
1/2 cup chopped walnuts or pecans (optional)

● DIRECTIONS PREP TIME | 15 MIN COOK TIME | 35 MIN

1 | Preheat the air fryer to 320°F (160°C). **2 |** Whisk together the flour, baking soda, and salt in a large bowl. **3 |** Cream the softened butter and brown sugar in a separate bowl until light and fluffy. **4 |** Beat in the eggs, one at a time, until well combined. Stir in the mashed bananas and vanilla extract until fully incorporated. **5 |** Gradually add the dry ingredients to the banana mixture, mixing until combined. Be careful not to overmix.
6 | Fold in the chopped nuts if using. **7 |** Grease a 7-inch round or square cake pan that fits into your air fryer basket. Pour the batter into the prepared pan and smooth the top. **8 |** Place the pan in the preheated air fryer and bake for 30-35 minutes, or until a toothpick inserted into the center of the bread comes out clean. **9 |** Allow the bread to cool in the pan for about 10 minutes before transferring it to a wire rack to cool completely.

CHOCOLATE **FANTASY CHEESECAKE**

● INGREDIENTS

For the crust:
1 1/2 cups of chocolate graham
cracker crumbs or crushed chocolate
cookies
1/4 cup granulated sugar
1/2 cup unsalted butter, melted
For the filling:
4 (8 oz) packages of cream cheese,
softened

1 1/4 cups granulated sugar
1/4 cup cocoa powder
8 oz semi-sweet chocolate, melted
and slightly cooled
1 teaspoon vanilla extract
4 large eggs
1 cup sour cream
1/2 cup heavy cream

● DIRECTIONS PREP TIME | 25 MIN COOK TIME | 50 MIN

1 | In a medium bowl, mix the chocolate graham cracker crumbs or crushed chocolate cookies, sugar, and melted butter until well combined. Press the mixture firmly into the bottom of a greased 7-inch springform pan. Place the pan in the refrigerator to chill while preparing the filling. **2 |** In a large bowl, beat the softened cream cheese until smooth and creamy. Gradually add the sugar and cocoa powder, and continue to beat until well combined. Mix in the melted chocolate and vanilla extract. **3 |** Add the eggs, one at a time, beating well after each addition. Add the sour and heavy cream, and mix until the batter is smooth and well combined. **4 |** Pour the filling over the prepared crust in the springform pan. Smooth the top with a spatula. **5 |** Preheat the air fryer to 325°F (165°C). **6 |** Place the springform pan in the preheated air fryer. Bake for 45-50 minutes until the edges are set and the center is slightly jiggly. Turn off the air fryer and let the cheesecake sit in it for 30 minutes. **7 |** Remove the cheesecake from the air fryer and let it cool at room temperature. Once cooled, refrigerate for at least 4 hours or overnight to set.

SILKY **SMOOTH CHOCOLATE INDULGENCE PIE**

● INGREDIENTS

1 pre-made pie crust
1/2 cup unsalted butter, softened
3/4 cup granulated sugar
2 ounces unsweetened chocolate,
melted and cooled

1 teaspoon vanilla extract
2 large eggs
Whipped cream for topping
Chocolate shavings for garnish

● DIRECTIONS PREP TIME | 20 MIN COOK TIME | 20 MIN

1 | Preheat the air fryer to 320°F (160°C). **2 |** Roll out the pre-made pie crust and place it in a small, air fryer-safe dish. **3 |** In a large bowl, beat the softened butter and granulated sugar until light and fluffy. Add the melted chocolate and vanilla extract, mixing until well combined.
4 | Add the eggs one at a time, beating for 3 minutes after each addition.
5 | Pour the chocolate mixture into the pie crust.
6 | Place the pie dish in the air fryer basket and cook for 15-20 minutes until the filling sets and the crust turns golden brown. **7 |** Remove the pie from the air fryer and let it cool before serving. Top with whipped cream and chocolate shavings.

CLASSIC **BUTTERMILK BISCUITS**

● INGREDIENTS 🥞 YIELDS | 8-10 BISCUITS

2 cups all-purpose flour
1 tablespoon baking powder
1/4 teaspoon baking soda
1 teaspoon salt

1/2 cup unsalted butter, icy and cut
into small pieces
3/4 cup cold buttermilk
1 tablespoon honey (optional)

● DIRECTIONS ⏱ PREP TIME | 20 MIN 🍳 COOK TIME | 12 MIN

1 | Whisk together the flour, baking powder, baking soda, and salt in a large bowl.
2 | Add the cold, cubed butter to the flour mixture. Cut the butter into the flour using a pastry cutter or fingers until the mixture resembles coarse crumbs. **3 |** Make a well in the center of the flour mixture and pour in the cold buttermilk and honey (if using). Stir until just combined, being careful not to overmix. The dough should be slightly sticky.
4 | Turn the dough onto a lightly floured surface and gently knead it until it comes together. Pat the dough into a 1-inch thick rectangle. **5 |** Fold the dough over on itself a few times (about 3-4 times) to create layers. Pat it back into a 1-inch thick rectangle.
6 | Using a biscuit or a round cookie cutter, cut out biscuits and place them in a greased air fryer basket. **7 |** Preheat the air fryer to 375°F (190°C). **8 |** Place the basket with the biscuits into the preheated air fryer and bake for 10-12 minutes or until golden brown and cooked. **9 |** Remove the biscuits from the air fryer and let them cool slightly before serving.

SAVORY CHEDDAR **BLISS BISCUITS**

● INGREDIENTS 🥞 YIELDS | 8-10 BISCUITS

2 cups all-purpose flour
1 tablespoon baking powder
1/4 teaspoon baking soda
1 teaspoon salt
1/2 cup unsalted butter, icy and cut
into small pieces

1 cup sharp cheddar cheese, grated
3/4 cup cold buttermilk
1 tablespoon honey (optional)

● DIRECTIONS ⏱ PREP TIME | 25 MIN 🍳 COOK TIME | 12 MIN

1 | Whisk together the flour, baking powder, baking soda, and salt in a large bowl.
2 | Add the cold, cubed butter to the flour mixture. Cut the butter into the flour using a pastry cutter or fingers until the mixture resembles coarse crumbs. **3 |** Mix in the grated cheddar cheese.
4 | Make a well in the center of the flour mixture and pour in the cold buttermilk and honey (if using). Stir until just combined, being careful not to overmix. The dough should be slightly sticky.
5 | Turn the dough onto a lightly floured surface and gently knead it until it comes together. Pat the dough into a 1-inch thick rectangle.
6 | Fold the dough over on itself a few times (about 3-4 times) to create layers. Pat it back into a 1-inch thick rectangle. **7 |** Using a biscuit or a round cookie cutter, cut out biscuits and place them in a greased air fryer basket. **8 |** Preheat the air fryer to 375°F (190°C). **9 |** Place the basket with the biscuits into the preheated air fryer and bake for 10-12 minutes or until golden brown and cooked. **10 |** Remove the biscuits from the air fryer and let them cool slightly before serving.

QUICHE **LORRAINE**

● **INGREDIENTS** 📚 **YIELDS | 6 SERVES**

For the crust:
1 1/2 cups all-purpose flour
1/2 teaspoon salt
1/2 cup unsalted butter, cold and cubed
3-4 tablespoons ice water
For the filling:
4 large eggs

1 cup heavy cream
1 cup milk
1/2 teaspoon salt
1/4 teaspoon ground black pepper
1/2 cup cooked and crumbled bacon
1/4 cup onions, finely chopped and sautéed
1 cup Swiss cheese, shredded

● **DIRECTIONS** ⏱ PREP TIME | 45 MIN 📟 COOK TIME | 40 MIN

1 | In a large bowl, mix the flour and salt. Cut in the cold butter until the mixture resembles coarse crumbs. Add one tablespoon of ice water until the dough comes together. Form the dough into a disk, wrap it in plastic wrap, and refrigerate for at least 30 minutes. **2 |** Roll out the dough on a lightly floured surface to fit a 7-inch (18 cm) springform pan or a similar air fryer-safe dish. Press the dough into the dish and trim the excess. Prick the bottom with a fork. **3 |** Line the crust with parchment paper and fill with pie weights or dried beans. Preheat the air fryer to 350°F (175°C). Place the crust in the air fryer and bake for 10 minutes. Remove the weights and parchment paper and bake for 5 minutes until the crust is golden. **4 |** Whisk together the eggs, heavy cream, milk, salt, and black pepper in a large bowl. **5 |** Evenly distribute the cooked bacon, sautéed onions, and shredded Swiss cheese over the baked crust. **6 |** Pour the egg mixture over the fillings in the crust. **7 |** Place the quiche in the air fryer and bake at 320°F (160°C) for 20-25 minutes until the filling sets and the top turns golden brown.
8 | Allow the quiche to cool for 10-15 minutes before removing it from the springform pan and slicing.

DECADENT **PECAN CARAMEL DREAM PIE**

● **INGREDIENTS** 📚 **YIELDS | 6-8 SLICES**

1 pre-made pie crust
1/2 cup corn syrup
1/2 cup granulated sugar
1/4 cup unsalted butter, melted
2 large eggs

1 cup pecan halves
1 teaspoon vanilla extract
1/4 teaspoon salt
1/4 cup caramel sauce

● **DIRECTIONS** ⏱ PREP TIME | 15 MIN 📟 COOK TIME | 25 MIN

1 | Preheat the air fryer to 320°F (160°C). **2 |** Roll out the pre-made pie crust and place it in a small, air fryer-safe dish. **3 |** In a large bowl, whisk together the corn syrup, granulated sugar, melted butter, eggs, vanilla extract, and salt until well combined.
4 | Stir in the pecan halves and caramel sauce. **5 |** Pour the pecan mixture into the pie crust. **6 |** Place the pie dish in the air fryer basket and cook for 20-25 minutes until the filling sets and the crust turns golden brown. **7 |** Remove the pie from the air fryer and let it cool before serving.

ULTIMATE CHOCOLATE CHIP DELIGHT COOKIES

● INGREDIENTS 🍪 YIELDS | 24 COOKIES

1 cup unsalted butter, softened
1 cup granulated sugar
1 cup brown sugar, packed
2 large eggs
2 teaspoons vanilla extract
3 cups all-purpose flour

1 teaspoon baking soda
1/2 teaspoon baking powder
1/2 teaspoon salt
2 cups semi-sweet chocolate chips
Cooking spray

● DIRECTIONS ⏱ PREP TIME | 15 MIN 🍳 COOK TIME | 10 MIN

1 | In a large mixing bowl, cream the softened butter, granulated sugar, and brown sugar until light and fluffy. Add the eggs one at a time, beating well after each addition, then mix in the vanilla extract. **2 |** Whisk together the all-purpose flour, baking soda, baking powder, and salt in a separate bowl. Gradually add the dry and wet ingredients, mixing until just combined. Stir in the semi-sweet chocolate chips until evenly distributed.
3 | Preheat the air fryer to 350°F (175°C). Lightly spray the air fryer basket with cooking spray.
4 | Scoop tablespoon-sized balls of dough and place them on parchment paper. Flatten the balls slightly with your fingers, then place the flattened dough balls in the prepared air fryer basket, spacing them about 2 inches apart. **5 |** Cook in the preheated air fryer for 8-10 minutes until the edges turn golden brown and the centers set. Allow the cookies to cool on the air fryer basket for 2 minutes before transferring them to a wire rack to cool completely.

HEAVENLY LEMON MERINGUE BLISS PIE

● INGREDIENTS 🍪 YIELDS | 6-8 SLICES

1 pre-made pie crust
1 cup granulated sugar
1/4 cup cornstarch
1/4 teaspoon salt
1 1/2 cups water
3 large egg yolks, beaten

2 tablespoons unsalted butter
1/4 cup fresh lemon juice
1 tablespoon lemon zest
3 large egg whites
1/4 teaspoon cream of tartar
1/4 cup granulated sugar

● DIRECTIONS ⏱ PREP TIME | 20 MIN 🍳 COOK TIME | 20 MIN

1 | Preheat the air fryer to 320°F (160°C). **2 |** Roll out the pre-made pie crust and place it in a small, air fryer-safe dish. **3 |** Combine the 1 cup granulated sugar, cornstarch, and salt in a saucepan. Gradually add water, stirring until smooth. Cook over medium heat, stirring constantly, until the mixture thickens and boils. **4 |** Stir a small amount of the hot mixture into the beaten egg yolks, then return the mixture to the saucepan. Cook for 2 minutes, stirring constantly. Remove from heat and stir in the butter, lemon juice, and lemon zest. **5 |** Pour the lemon filling into the pie crust. **6 |** In a large bowl, beat the egg whites and cream of tartar until soft peaks form. Gradually add the 1/4 cup granulated sugar, beating until stiff peaks form. Spread the meringue over the lemon filling, sealing the edges to the crust. **7 |** Place the pie dish in the air fryer basket and cook for 15-20 minutes or until the meringue is golden brown. **8 |** Remove the pie from the air fryer and let it cool before serving.

CRUNCHY CINNAMON **DELIGHT CHURROS**

● **INGREDIENTS** YIELDS | 20 CHURROS

1 cup water
1/2 cup unsalted butter
1 tablespoon granulated sugar
1/4 teaspoon salt
1 cup all-purpose flour

3 large eggs
1 teaspoon vanilla extract
Cooking spray
1/2 cup granulated sugar
1 teaspoon ground cinnamon

● **DIRECTIONS** PREP TIME | 20 MIN COOK TIME | 10 MIN

1 | Combine water, butter, sugar, and salt in a medium saucepan. Bring to a boil over medium heat. Reduce heat to low and add the flour all at once, stirring vigorously until the mixture forms a ball and pulls away from the sides of the pan. Remove from heat and let cool for 5 minutes.
2 | Add eggs one at a time, beating well after each addition until the dough is smooth and glossy. Stir in the vanilla extract. **3 |** Preheat your air fryer to 375°F (190°C). Transfer the dough to a piping bag fitted with a star tip. Pipe the dough into 4-inch strips onto a parchment paper-lined tray. Spray the churros lightly with cooking spray. **4 |** Place the churros in the air fryer basket in a single layer, ensuring they do not touch. Air fry for 8-10 minutes, flipping halfway through, until golden brown and crispy. **5 |** In a shallow dish, mix the granulated sugar and ground cinnamon. Immediately roll the hot churros in the cinnamon-sugar mixture to coat.
6 | Serve warm with chocolate sauce or your favorite dipping sauce.

GOLDEN **DELIGHT DONUTS**

● **INGREDIENTS** YIELDS | 12 DONUTS

1 cup whole milk, warmed (110°F or 43°C)
1/4 cup granulated sugar
2 1/4 teaspoons active dry yeast (1 packet)
2 large eggs, room temperature
1/2 cup unsalted butter, melted
1 teaspoon vanilla extract

4 cups all-purpose flour
1/2 teaspoon salt
Cooking spray
1/2 cup melted butter (for coating)
1 cup granulated sugar mixed with 1
teaspoon ground cinnamon (for coating)

● **DIRECTIONS** PREP TIME | 1 HOUR 30 MIN COOK TIME | 6 MIN

1 | In a large bowl, combine warm milk and granulated sugar. Sprinkle the yeast over the milk and let it sit for 5-10 minutes until foamy. **2 |** Add eggs, melted butter, and vanilla extract to the yeast mixture. Stir to combine. **3 |** In a separate bowl, whisk together the flour and salt. Gradually add the flour mixture to the wet ingredients, stirring until a dough forms. Knead the dough on a lightly floured surface for 5-7 minutes until smooth and elastic. **4 |** Place the dough in a greased bowl, cover, and let it rise in a warm place for about 1 hour or until doubled in size. **5 |** Once the dough has risen, roll it out on a floured surface to about 1/2-inch thickness. Use a donut cutter or two different-sized round cutters to cut out the donuts and donut holes. **6 |** Preheat the air fryer to 375°F (190°C). Lightly spray the air fryer basket with cooking spray. Place the donuts in the air fryer basket in a single layer, ensuring they do not touch. **7 |** Air fry the donuts for 5-6 minutes, flipping halfway through, until golden brown. Brush the hot donuts with melted butter and roll them in the cinnamon-sugar mixture to coat.

CINNAMON **APPLE DELIGHT FRITTERS**

● INGREDIENTS 　YIELDS | 12 FRITTERS

1 cup all-purpose flour
1/4 cup granulated sugar
1 teaspoon baking powder
1/2 teaspoon ground cinnamon
1/4 teaspoon salt
1/4 cup milk
1 large egg
1 teaspoon vanilla extract

1 tablespoon unsalted butter, melted
2 medium apples, peeled, cored, and diced
Cooking spray
1/2 cup powdered sugar
1-2 tablespoons milk (for glaze)
1/2 teaspoon vanilla extract (for glaze)

● DIRECTIONS 　PREP TIME | 20 MIN 　COOK TIME | 10 MIN

1 | Whisk together the flour, granulated sugar, baking powder, ground cinnamon, and salt in a large bowl. **2 |** Mix the milk, egg, vanilla extract, and melted butter in a separate bowl until well combined. Add the wet ingredients to the dry ingredients and stir until just combined. Fold in the diced apples. **3 |** Preheat the air fryer to 375°F (190°C). Line the air fryer basket with parchment paper and lightly spray with cooking spray. **4 |** Drop spoonfuls of the apple fritter batter onto the parchment paper, spacing them apart to avoid touching. Air fry the fritters for 8-10 minutes, flipping halfway through, until golden brown and cooked through. **5 |** While the fritters cook, prepare the glaze by mixing the powdered sugar, milk, and vanilla extract in a small bowl until smooth. **6 |** Once the fritters are cooked, let them cool slightly on a wire rack. Drizzle the glaze over the warm fritters.

CHOCOLATE **DREAM CROISSANTS**

● INGREDIENTS 　YIELDS | 8 CROISSANTS

1 sheet puff pastry, thawed
1/2 cup semi-sweet chocolate chips or chopped chocolate

1 egg, beaten (for egg wash)
Powdered sugar (for dusting)

● DIRECTIONS 　PREP TIME | 15 MIN 　COOK TIME | 10 MIN

1 | Whisk together the flour, granulated sugar, baking powder, ground cinnamon, and salt in a large bowl.
2 | Mix the milk, egg, vanilla extract, and melted butter in a separate bowl until well combined. Add the wet ingredients to the dry ingredients and stir until just combined. Fold in the diced apples.
3 | Preheat the air fryer to 375°F (190°C). Line the air fryer basket with parchment paper and lightly spray with cooking spray.
4 | Drop spoonfuls of the apple fritter batter onto the parchment paper, spacing them apart to avoid touching. Air fry the fritters for 8-10 minutes, flipping halfway through, until golden brown and cooked through.
5 | While the fritters cook, prepare the glaze by mixing the powdered sugar, milk, and vanilla extract in a small bowl until smooth.
6 | Once the fritters are cooked, let them cool slightly on a wire rack. Drizzle the glaze over the warm fritters.

CHOCOLATE **CHIP DREAM MUFFINS**

● **INGREDIENTS** 🥞 YIELDS | 12 MUFFINS

1 3/4 cups all-purpose flour
3/4 cup granulated sugar
1/2 teaspoon salt
1 1/2 teaspoons baking powder
1/4 teaspoon baking soda

1/3 cup vegetable oil
1 large egg
3/4 cup milk
1 teaspoon vanilla extract
1 cup semi-sweet chocolate chips

● **DIRECTIONS** ⏱ PREP TIME | 15 MIN 🍳 COOK TIME | 25 MIN

1 | Preheat the oven to 375°F (190°C). Line a muffin tin with paper liners.
2 | Combine the flour, sugar, salt, baking powder, and baking soda in a large bowl.
3 | Whisk together the vegetable oil, egg, milk, and vanilla extract in a medium bowl.
4 | Add the wet ingredients to the dry ingredients and mix until just combined.
5 | Gently fold in the chocolate chips.
6 | Divide the batter evenly among the 12 muffin cups, filling each about 2/3 full.
7 | Bake for 20-25 minutes, or until a toothpick inserted into the center of a muffin comes out clean.
8 | Remove from the oven and let cool in the muffin tin for 5 minutes, then transfer to a wire rack to cool completely.

BURSTING **BLUEBERRY BLISS MUFFINS**

● **INGREDIENTS** 🥞 YIELDS | 12 MUFFINS

1 3/4 cups all-purpose flour
1/2 cup granulated sugar
1/2 teaspoon salt
1 1/2 teaspoons baking powder
1/4 teaspoon baking soda
1/3 cup vegetable oil

1 large egg
3/4 cup milk
1 teaspoon vanilla extract
1 cup fresh or frozen blueberries
2 tablespoons all-purpose flour (for coating blueberries)

● **DIRECTIONS** ⏱ PREP TIME | 15 MIN 🍳 COOK TIME | 25 MIN

1 | Preheat the oven to 375°F (190°C). Line a muffin tin with paper liners.
2 | In a large bowl, combine 1 3/4 cups flour, sugar, salt, baking powder, and baking soda.
3 | Whisk together the vegetable oil, egg, milk, and vanilla extract in a medium bowl.
4 | Add the wet ingredients to the dry ingredients and mix until just combined.
5 | Coat the blueberries with 2 tablespoons of flour in a small bowl. This technique helps prevent the mix-ins from sinking to the bottom of the muffins.
6 | Gently fold the coated blueberries into the batter.
7 | Divide the batter evenly among the 12 muffin cups, filling each about 2/3 full.
8 | Bake for 20-25 minutes, or until a toothpick inserted into the center of a muffin comes out clean.
9 | Remove from the oven and let cool in the muffin tin for 5 minutes, then transfer to a wire rack to cool completely.

VARIETY PRETZELS

● **INGREDIENTS** 🍽 **YIELDS | 8 PRETZELS OR 32 PRETZEL BITES**

1 1/2 cups warm water (110°F/45°C)
1 packet active dry yeast (2 1/4 teaspoons)
1 tablespoon granulated sugar
4 cups all-purpose flour
1 teaspoon salt
For the boiling solution:
1/4 cup baking soda
4 cups boiling water

For Cheddar Pretzels:
1 cup shredded cheddar cheese
Coarse salt for sprinkling
For Cinnamon Sugar Pretzels:
1/4 cup melted butter
1/2 cup granulated sugar
2 teaspoons ground cinnamon

● **DIRECTIONS** ⏱ **PREP TIME | 20 MIN** 🍳 **COOK TIME | 12 MIN**

1 | In a large bowl, dissolve the yeast and 1 tablespoon of granulated sugar in warm water. Let it sit for 5 minutes until it becomes frothy. **2 |** Add the flour and salt to the yeast mixture. For cheddar pretzels, add shredded cheddar cheese. Knead until a smooth dough forms. **3 |** Divide the dough into 8 equal pieces. Roll each piece into a long rope and shape it into a pretzel, or cut the dough into small bite-sized pieces for pretzel bites. **4 |** In a shallow pan, dissolve the baking soda in 4 cups of boiling water. Dip each pretzel or pretzel bite into the solution for about 10-15 seconds and place them on a parchment-lined air fryer basket. **5 |** Preheat the air fryer to 375°F (190°C).
6 | *For Cheddar Pretzels:* Sprinkle the pretzels or pretzel bites with coarse salt.
7 | Place the basket with the pretzels or bites in the preheated air fryer. Bake for 10-12 minutes for pretzels and 8-10 minutes for pretzel bites, or until golden brown.
8 | *For Cinnamon Sugar Pretzels*, brush the pretzels with melted butter while they are still warm. In a small bowl, mix the granulated sugar and ground cinnamon. Sprinkle the cinnamon-sugar mixture over the buttered pretzels or pretzel bites.

CLASSIC SAUSAGE ROLLS

● **INGREDIENTS** 🍽 **YIELDS | 12 SAUSAGE ROLLS**

1 lb ground sausage (mild or spicy)
1 sheet puff pastry, thawed
1 egg, beaten (for egg wash)

1 tablespoon mustard (optional)
1/2 teaspoon black pepper

● **DIRECTIONS** ⏱ **PREP TIME | 15 MIN** 🍳 **COOK TIME | 15 MIN**

1 | Roll out the puff pastry sheet on a lightly floured surface. **2 |** Mix the ground sausage with black pepper and mustard (if using). **3 |** Spread the sausage mixture in a long line down the center of the pastry sheet. **4 |** Roll the pastry over the sausage mixture to form a log, sealing the edges with beaten egg. **5 |** Cut the log into 2-inch pieces and place them in the air fryer basket.
6 | Brush the tops with the remaining beaten egg.
7 | Preheat the air fryer to 375°F (190°C). **8 |** Preheat the air fryer, put the basket inside, and bake for 12-15 minutes until the pastry turns golden brown and the sausage cooks through. **9 |** Allow the sausage rolls to cool slightly before serving.

UNIVERSAL EMPANADAS RECIPE

● INGREDIENTS 🥞 YIELDS | 12 EMPANADAS

Dough Ingredients:
2 1/2 cups all-purpose flour
1 teaspoon salt
1/2 cup unsalted butter, cold and cubed
1 egg
1/3 cup ice water
1 tablespoon vinegar
Filling Options:
Beef Filling:
1/2 lb ground beef
1 small onion, finely chopped
1 clove garlic, minced
1/2 teaspoon ground cumin
Salt and pepper to taste
1/4 cup tomato sauce
1/4 cup chopped green olives (optional)
Chicken Filling:
1/2 lb cooked chicken, shredded
1/2 small onion, finely chopped

1/2 teaspoon ground cumin
1/2 teaspoon smoked paprika
Salt and pepper to taste
1/4 cup chicken broth
1/4 cup chopped green olives (optional)
Cheese Filling:
1 cup shredded mozzarella or cheddar cheese
1/4 cup cream cheese
1/2 teaspoon garlic powder
1/2 teaspoon dried oregano
Ham and Cheese Filling:
1/2 cup diced ham
1 cup shredded cheddar cheese
1/4 cup cream cheese
Spinach and Cheese Filling:
1 cup fresh spinach, chopped
1/2 cup feta cheese, crumbled
1/4 cup cream cheese
1 clove garlic, minced

● DIRECTIONS  PREP TIME | 45 MIN  COOK TIME | 12 MIN

1 | In a large bowl, whisk together the flour and salt. Cut in the cold butter until the mixture resembles coarse crumbs.

2 | In a small bowl, beat the egg with the ice water and vinegar. Pour the wet ingredients into the flour mixture and mix until just combined. Form the dough into a disk, wrap it in plastic wrap, and refrigerate for at least 30 minutes.

3 | Prepare the fillings:

Beef Filling: In a skillet, cook the ground beef, onion, and garlic until browned. Drain excess fat. Add cumin, salt, pepper, tomato sauce, and olives. Cook for another 5 minutes. Let cool.

Chicken Filling: In a skillet, cook the onion until softened. Add shredded chicken, cumin, smoked paprika, salt, pepper, chicken broth, and olives. Cook for 5 minutes. Let cool. **Cheese Filling:** Mix shredded cheese, cream cheese, garlic powder, and oregano in a bowl. **Ham and Cheese Filling:** Mix diced ham, shredded cheese, and cream cheese in a bowl. **Spinach and Cheese Filling:** In a skillet, cook the garlic until fragrant. Add chopped spinach and cook until wilted. Mix with feta and cream cheese. Let cool.

4 | On a lightly floured surface, roll out the dough to about 1/8-inch thickness. Cut out circles using a 4-inch round cutter. **5 |** Place 1-2 tablespoons of filling in the center of each dough circle. Fold the dough to form a half-moon shape, pressing the edges together to seal. Crimp the edges with a fork. **6 |** Preheat the air fryer to 375°F (190°C).

7 | Brush the empanadas with a beaten egg for a golden finish. Place the empanadas in a single layer in the air fryer basket, ensuring they are not touching. **8 |** Air fry the empanadas for 10-12 minutes until golden brown and crispy. **9 |** Allow the empanadas to cool for a few minutes before serving.

SPINACH **AND FETA QUICHE**

● **INGREDIENTS** 🍶 YIELDS | 6 SERVES

For the crust:
1 1/2 cups all-purpose flour
1/2 teaspoon salt
1/2 cup unsalted butter, cold and cubed
3-4 tablespoons ice water
For the filling:
4 large eggs

1 cup heavy cream
1 cup milk
1/2 teaspoon salt
1/4 teaspoon ground black pepper
1 cup fresh spinach, chopped
1/2 cup crumbled feta cheese
1/4 cup onions, finely chopped and sautéed

● **DIRECTIONS** ⏱ PREP TIME | 45 MIN 🍳 COOK TIME | 40 MIN

1 | In a large bowl, mix the flour and salt. Cut in the cold butter until the mixture resembles coarse crumbs. Add one tablespoon of ice water until the dough comes together. Form the dough into a disk, wrap it in plastic wrap, and refrigerate for at least 30 minutes.

2 | Roll out the dough on a lightly floured surface to fit a 7-inch (18 cm) springform pan or a similar air fryer-safe dish. Press the dough into the dish and trim the excess. Prick the bottom with a fork.

3 | Line the crust with parchment paper and fill with pie weights or dried beans. Preheat the air fryer to 350°F (175°C). Place the crust in the air fryer and bake for 10 minutes. Remove the weights and parchment paper and bake for 5 minutes until the crust is golden.

4 | Whisk together the eggs, heavy cream, milk, salt, and black pepper in a large bowl.

5 | Evenly distribute the chopped spinach, crumbled feta cheese, and sautéed onions over the baked crust.

6 | Pour the egg mixture over the fillings in the crust.

7 | Preheat the air fryer to 320°F (160°C), place the quiche inside, and bake for 20-25 minutes until the filling sets and the top turns golden brown.

8 | Allow the quiche to cool for 10-15 minutes before removing it from the springform pan and slicing.

UNIVERSAL **EGG ROLLS RECIPE**

 **INGREDIENTS** **YIELDS | 12 EGG ROLLS**

Ingredients for the Wrapper:
12 egg roll wrappers
1 egg, beaten (for sealing)
Filling Options:
Pork and Cabbage Filling:
1/2 lb ground pork
1 cup shredded cabbage
1/2 cup shredded carrots
2 cloves garlic, minced
1 tablespoon soy sauce
1 teaspoon grated ginger
Salt and pepper to taste
Chicken and Vegetable Filling:
1/2 lb cooked chicken, shredded
1 cup shredded cabbage
1/2 cup shredded carrots
1/2 cup bell peppers, thinly sliced
2 cloves garlic, minced
1 tablespoon soy sauce
Salt and pepper to taste
Shrimp and Vegetable Filling:
1/2 lb cooked shrimp, chopped

1 cup shredded cabbage
1/2 cup shredded carrots
1/2 cup bean sprouts
2 cloves garlic, minced
1 tablespoon soy sauce
Salt and pepper to taste
Vegetarian Filling:
1 cup shredded cabbage
1/2 cup shredded carrots
1/2 cup mushrooms, thinly sliced
1/2 cup bell peppers, thinly sliced
1/2 cup bean sprouts
2 cloves garlic, minced
1 tablespoon soy sauce
Salt and pepper to taste
Philly Cheesesteak Filling:
1/2 lb sliced steak
1/2 cup bell peppers, thinly sliced
1/2 cup onions, thinly sliced
1 cup shredded provolone cheese
Salt and pepper to taste

 **DIRECTIONS**  **PREP TIME | 30 MIN** **COOK TIME | 10 MIN**

1 | For each filling, heat a skillet over medium heat and cook the meat (if uncooked) until browned. Add the vegetables and cook until softened. Add garlic, soy sauce, and other seasonings, and cook for 2-3 minutes. Remove from heat and let the filling cool slightly.

2 | Lay an egg roll wrapper on a clean surface with one corner pointing towards you (diamond shape). Place 2-3 tablespoons of filling near the center of the wrapper. Fold the bottom corner over the filling, then fold in the sides. Brush the top corner with the beaten egg and roll tightly to seal.

3 | Preheat the air fryer to 375°F (190°C).

4 | Place the egg rolls in the air fryer basket in a single layer, ensuring they are not touching. Lightly spray or brush the egg rolls with oil.

5 | Air fry for 8-10 minutes, turning halfway through, until they are golden brown and crispy. Allow the egg rolls to cool for a few minutes before serving. Serve with your favorite dipping sauces.

UNIVERSAL **PIZZA ROLLS RECIPE**

● INGREDIENTS  YIELDS | 24 PIZZA ROLLS

Dough Ingredients:
2 1/4 teaspoons active dry yeast
1 cup warm water (110°F/45°C)
1 tablespoon granulated sugar
2 tablespoons olive oil
3 cups all-purpose flour
1 teaspoon salt

Filling Options:
Classic Pepperoni Filling:
1 cup shredded mozzarella cheese
1/2 cup sliced pepperoni
1/4 cup pizza sauce

Cheese Filling:
1 1/2 cups shredded mozzarella cheese
1/4 cup grated Parmesan cheese
1/4 cup pizza sauce

Sausage Filling:
1 cup cooked and crumbled Italian sausage

1 cup shredded mozzarella cheese
1/4 cup pizza sauce

Vegetarian Filling:
1/2 cup diced bell peppers
1/2 cup sliced mushrooms
1/2 cup chopped spinach
1 cup shredded mozzarella cheese
1/4 cup pizza sauce

Supreme Filling:
1/2 cup cooked and crumbled Italian sausage
1/2 cup sliced pepperoni
1/4 cup diced onions
1/4 cup diced bell peppers
1 cup shredded mozzarella cheese
1/4 cup pizza sauce

● DIRECTIONS  PREP TIME | 1 HOUR 30 MIN ⬜ COOK TIME | 12 MIN

1 | In a large bowl, dissolve the yeast and sugar in warm water. Let it sit for 5 minutes until frothy.
2 | Add olive oil, flour, and salt to the yeast mixture. Mix until the dough comes together, then knead the dough on a lightly floured surface for 5-7 minutes until smooth and elastic.
3 | Put the dough in a greased bowl, cover it with a damp cloth, and let it rise in a warm place for about 1 hour or until it doubles in size.
4 | Punch down the dough and roll it out on a lightly floured surface into a large rectangle. Spread a thin layer of pizza sauce over the rolled-out dough, leaving a 1-inch border around the edges. Sprinkle the chosen filling ingredients evenly over the sauce.
5 | Roll the dough tightly into a log from the long side. Pinch the seams and ends to seal. Cut the rolled dough into 1-inch (2.54 cm) pieces and place them in the air fryer basket, ensuring they are not touching.
6 | Preheat the air fryer to 375°F (190°C). Put the basket in the preheated air fryer and bake for 10-12 minutes until the pizza rolls turn golden brown and cook through.
7 | Allow the pizza rolls to cool for a few minutes before serving.

INDEX

Monterey Jack cheese
Quick Enchilada Delight,28
Loaded Nachos,87
Southwest Egg Rolls,98

O

onion
Loaded Breakfast Burritos,12
Golden Hash Browns,13
Cheesy Veggie Bagels,18
Mexican Chicken Fajitas,36
Argentine Chicken Empanadas,37
Crispy Onion Rings,69
Rainbow Veggie Skewers,72
Sweet and Spicy Meatballs,95
Quick Enchilada Delight,28
Quiche Lorraine,106

P

Parmesan cheese
Cheddar Morning Soufflés,21
Parmesan-Crusted Chicken Thighs,29
Italian Chicken Rolls,29
Classic Turkey Meatballs,31
Crispy Pork Chops,44
Garlic Parmesan Tenderloin,46
Golden Pork Schnitzel,46
Juicy Pork Meatballs,48
Meat Stuffed Mushrooms,52
Crispy Salmon Fillets,54
Herb-Crusted Sea Bass,57
Garlic Parmesan Shrimp,59
Lemon-Garlic Stuffed Sea Bass,62
Italian Herb-Crusted Flounder,67
Parmesan Crusted Cauliflower Bites,69
Stuffed Cream Cheese Mushrooms,73
Cheesy Cauliflower Balls,74
Parmesan Zucchini Sticks,74
Zucchini Fritters,75
Cheesy Potato Croquettes,76
Parmesan Broccoli Steaks,77
Cauliflower and Broccoli Patties,78
Universal Pizza Rolls Recipe,115

peanut butter
Energizing Granola Balls,19
Thai Peanut Chicken Skewers,31
Thai Chicken Satay,38
Peanut Butter Swirl Brownies,100

pecan
Decadent Pecan Caramel Dream Pie,106
Maple Pecan Oatmeal,23
Sticky Pecan Bliss Rolls,103
Ultimate Banana Bliss Bread,103

pepperoni
Variety Mini Pizzas,85
Universal Pizza Rolls Recipe,115

pesto sauce
Pesto Fish Rolls,61

phyllo pastry
Mini Philly Cheesesteak Bites,96

pie crust
Irresistible Pumpkin Spice Delight Pie,99
Caramel Apple Crumble Pie,101
Silky Smooth Chocolate Indulgence Pie,104
Decadent Pecan Caramel Dream Pie,106
Heavenly Lemon Meringue Bliss Pie,107

pineapple
Pork Tacos with Pineapple Salsa,49
Shrimp Pineapple Rolls,63

pita
Red Pepper Hummus,94

pizza crust
Brunch Pizza Delight,24
Variety Mini Pizzas,85

pizza dough
Meat Lover's Pizza,51

pizza sauce
Meat Lover's Pizza,51
Variety Mini Pizzas,85
Universal Pizza Rolls Recipe,115

pork
Savory Sausage Patties,13
Quick & Savory Meatloaf,41
Pork & Apple Skewers,48
Juicy Pork Meatballs,48
Pork Tacos with Pineapple Salsa,49
Meat Lover's Egg Rolls,50
Stuffed Bell Peppers,51
Meat Stuffed Mushrooms,52
Classic Chili Con Carne,53
Variety Deep-Fried Sandwiches,86
Variety Spring Rolls,89
Sweet and Spicy Meatballs,95
Universal Egg Rolls Recipe,114

pork belly
Maple Glazed Pork Belly,47

pork chops
Golden Pork Schnitzel,46

pork ribs
Sweet & Tangy BBQ Ribs,45

pork shoulder
Pulled Pork Sliders,45

pork tenderloin
Garlic Parmesan Tenderloin,46

potatoes
Crispy Breakfast Potatoes,11
Golden Hash Browns,13
Ultimate Sweet Potato Fries Trio,68
Cheesy Potato Croquettes,76
Twice-Baked Potatoes,78
Loaded Potato Skins,87